Business Associations and Relationships

A Practical Introduction to Business Organization Law

JORDAN K. FAIRFIELD

Cover art by Getcovers

CONTENTS

CONTENTS

1 INTRODUCTION

Every business story begins with people trying to work together. Sometimes it's two friends starting a bakery out of a shared dream. Sometimes it's a sprawling corporation with thousands of shareholders scattered across the world. In every case, the moment people decide to join forces for a shared economic purpose, the law steps quietly onto the stage. It shapes who has the power to act, who bears the risk when things go wrong, whose promises matter, and whose choices bind the rest of the group. Yet few people—students, lawyers, or business owners—ever stop to ask the deeper questions: What actually turns a simple handshake into a legal partnership? Why is a corporation treated as a person separate from the humans who built it? How can someone be responsible for a contract they never signed, or for a wrong they didn't personally commit? Why are some business owners shielded from liability while others stand fully exposed? And what happens when someone misuses the very structure meant to protect them?

These questions are not just technical puzzles. They go to the heart of how we organize economic life. They reveal a world full of hidden assumptions—about authority, trust, responsibility, and fairness—that shapes nearly every transaction in modern society. This book is your guide to that world. It is designed to make these rules not only understandable, but genuinely interesting, alive with stories and examples that show how the law responds when ambition, conflict, cooperation, and risk collide.

The book is especially useful in three settings. First, it is designed as a complete study companion for the NextGen Uniform Bar Exam. The structure of the text mirrors the exam's scope topic by topic, making it an ideal resource for bar preparation. It is equally well suited for preparing for a typical law school final exam in Business Associations. The goal is clarity: to present each doctrine in a way that makes exam questions feel less like riddles and more like logical extensions of ideas you already understand. Second, the book can serve as an accessible introduction at the beginning of a Business Associations course or even at the start of law school itself. Many students find the subject challenging because it introduces unfamiliar vocabulary and unfamiliar relationships all at once—agency, partnerships, corporations, fiduciary duties, derivative suits, and more. This book gives you a framework before you encounter the technical details, so that when you dive deeper in class, the terrain already feels familiar. And third, this book is written for people with no legal background at all. If you are simply curious about how businesses are structured, why liability works the way it does, how partnerships differ from corporations or LLCs, or why courts sometimes "pierce" the veil of limited liability, this text is meant for you. It assumes no prior training, uses clear explanations, and builds each concept step by step.

Whether you are studying for an exam, preparing for a semester, or reading out of personal interest, you will find that business law is not just a set of rules—it is a story about how people shape their economic relationships, and how the law helps those relationships succeed or falter. Each chapter invites you to explore the moments when trust is tested, when responsibility shifts, when authority expands or collapses, and when the law must step in to resolve confusion or conflict. As you move through the chapters, you will discover how the pieces fit together: how agency lays the foundation for authority, how vicarious liability assigns responsibility, how partnerships and corporations channel power, how fiduciary duties maintain integrity, how litigation enforces accountability, and how liability rules define the boundary between the individual and the enterprise.

The questions we start with—who can act, who must answer, who gets to decide, and who bears the cost—become clearer with each chapter. By the end of the book, you will not only understand the rules but see how they operate in real life, how they rise to meet predictable conflicts, and how they quietly guide the behavior of millions of businesses every day. The law of business associations may at first seem abstract, but it is in fact the legal infrastructure of cooperation. And once you understand it, the business world looks different: more structured, more logical, and more deeply shaped by human choices than it first appears.

Welcome to the study of business associations. Let's begin.

2 AGENCY AND AUTHORITY

Agency law begins with the idea that one person can act for another in a way that changes the world around them. This simple idea has shaped business, government, and daily life for centuries. It allows large organizations to function and lets ordinary people delegate important tasks. But it also creates danger, because when a principal hands authority to an agent, even in small ways, the principal may be bound by what the agent does. A thoughtless promise, a misleading title, or a careless silence can tie a principal to a contract or expose them to liability they never imagined. The stories in agency law are filled with agents who exceeded their instructions, principals who failed to protect themselves, and third parties who acted on appearances that later turned out to be false. Understanding how these stories unfold is essential for mastering agency law and recognizing how it controls so many interactions in business.

Creation of Agency Relationship

Every agency relationship begins with three elements. First, the principal must manifest that the agent will act on the principal's behalf. Second, the agent must accept the assignment. Third, the principal must have the right to control the agent's actions. These elements do not require formal documents or official titles. They can arise from a handshake, a casual arrangement, or a role someone steps into without realizing the consequences. What matters is the meeting of minds between principal and agent and the presence of control. Control is the heart of agency. If the principal cannot direct the agent's actions, then the relationship is not an agency relationship, no matter how close the parties may be.

Sometimes agencies arise from unexpected places. A professor teaching a business organizations class does not create an agency relationship with her students because she does not authorize them to act on her behalf and they do not agree to do so. When that same professor hires a student as a research assistant, the analysis changes, but only slightly. In most universities, the research assistant is an employee of the institution, not of the professor. This means both the professor and the assistant are agents of the university. In that situation, the professor remains a superior co-agent with the right to direct the assistant's work, while the student is a subordinate co-agent. But neither acts as the principal of the other, because the university, not the professor, created the employment relationship.

In business settings, creation of agency is often clearer. When a company hires a salesperson, appoints a manager, or designates someone to represent it at a closing, those roles are usually accompanied by authority. Even so, courts do not look at the title alone. They look for manifestations from the principal and acceptance by the agent. This requirement ensures that agency cannot be created accidentally in situations where the parties have no intention of creating a binding relationship. At the same time, courts understand that manifestations can be subtle, and acceptance can be implied through behavior. It is this flexibility that allows agency law to fit so many situations.

Authority of the Agent to Bind the Principal

Once an agency relationship exists, the next question is the scope of the agent's authority. Authority determines when a principal is bound to a contract or legal obligation created by the agent. The law divides authority into two main categories: actual authority and apparent authority. Actual authority focuses on what the principal actually gave the agent, while apparent authority focuses on what third parties reasonably believe the agent possesses based on the principal's conduct.

Actual Authority

Actual authority arises from the exchanges between the principal and the agent. It exists when the principal tells the agent what they may do, either directly or implicitly. Express actual authority occurs when the principal uses words giving the agent permission to act. If a landscaping company owner tells an employee, "Go to the nursery and buy plants for the Johnson job," that is express authority. Implied actual authority arises from what is reasonably necessary to carry out the assigned task. If the same employee must charge the plants to the company's account or arrange transportation to deliver them, those actions may fall within implied authority.

Actual authority can be broad or narrow. It can be revoked, limited, or expanded at any time by the principal. In *Elting v. Elting*, the partners had adopted a partnership agreement that placed limits on their actual authority. One partner, Kerwin, entered into risky commodity contracts that caused losses of more than two million dollars. The other partners argued he lacked actual authority because the partnership agreement required majority approval for such transactions. The court agreed that he lacked actual authority. This illustrates how internal agreements and instructions define the actual authority of agents, especially in the partnership context, where each partner is otherwise presumed to have authority in the ordinary course of business. Actual authority depends on the principal's manifestations, and here those manifestations were found in the partnership agreement itself.

Apparent Authority

Apparent authority focuses on what third parties reasonably believe. A principal may be bound by an agent's actions even when the agent had no actual authority, if the principal made manifestations that caused the third party to believe the agent was authorized. In other words, the appearance of authority can become as powerful as authority itself. This doctrine reflects fairness toward third parties who act in reliance on the principal's conduct.

In *H.H. Taylor v. Ramsay–Gerding Construction*, a ChemRex territory manager visited a construction site, spoke with customers, and discussed warranty information. ChemRex gave him the title "territory manager," allowed him to process warranties, and placed him in direct contact with customers. When he promised that a stucco system was "bulletproof" and carried a five-year warranty, he exceeded his actual authority. But the court found that he had apparent authority, because ChemRex's own actions created the reasonable belief that he could speak about warranties. The company had clothed him with the appearance of authority. Because the customer relied on that appearance, ChemRex became bound to the promise even though it had never approved such a warranty.

A more down-to-earth example appears in the hypotheticals involving Scissorhands Landscaping. When Ryder, a new employee, arrived at a nursery driving a truck painted with "Scissorhands Landscaping," the nursery reasonably believed she had authority to charge plants to the company account. The employer had told her she was not authorized to charge anything, but the company's own manifestation—the branded truck—created the appearance of authority. Even though Ryder lacked actual authority, the company could still be bound. This illustrates how apparent authority can arise when a principal creates circumstances that cause others to believe the agent is authorized.

Apparent authority can also vanish. If a principal clearly notifies third parties that an agent lacks authority, or if the third party knows of the limitation, then apparent authority cannot exist. In one variation of the Scissorhands hypothetical, the nursery called to ask whether Ryder had authority to charge items. Scissorhands listened to the voicemail but failed to return the call. This silence raised the issue of estoppel, a related doctrine, but also showed how apparent authority can persist when the principal does not clarify the limits on an agent's power. When the principal fails to act in the face of uncertainty, the law may protect third parties who rely on what they see.

Fiduciary Duties of Agents to Principals

Agency law is not only about the power agents hold. It is also about the responsibilities that come with that power. Agents owe fiduciary duties to their principals. These duties ensure that agents act in the principal's interests rather than their own and that they use the authority given to them in a trustworthy and responsible manner. Two main fiduciary duties dominate this area: the duty of care and the duty of loyalty.

Duty of Care

The duty of care requires an agent to act with the reasonable skill, competence, and diligence that a prudent agent would use in similar circumstances. This duty requires agents to perform their tasks carefully, avoid reckless behavior, and take reasonable steps to protect the principal's interests. If an agent is hired because of a special skill or expertise, that higher standard becomes part of the duty of care.

In business relationships, the duty of care often appears when an agent fails to investigate important facts or proceeds with a transaction without adequate attention. For example, in Elting v. Elting, the court noted that partners should more carefully monitor partnership activities, especially when a partner engages in complex or risky transactions. Although the case turned on authority rather than breach of duty, the court's comments reflected the ongoing expectation that agents must act with reasonable diligence in business operations.

Duty of Loyalty

The duty of loyalty is far more dramatic. It requires the agent to put the principal's interests above their own in matters connected to the agency. Agents must not compete with their principals, must not use the principal's property or information for personal benefit, and must disclose relevant information. Any secret profit or hidden opportunity can violate this duty.

The story of *Foodcomm International v. Barry* shows how seriously the law takes loyalty. Two senior sales representatives at Foodcomm began planning a competing business while still employed by Foodcomm. They contacted one of Foodcomm's customers and asked whether the customer would shift its business to their new company. They even used Foodcomm's computers and devices to prepare the new business plan. Only after securing the customer's interest did they resign from Foodcomm. The court held that they had breached the duty of loyalty. The key point was that agents must terminate the agency relationship before pursuing competing opportunities. So long as they remain agents, their loyalty must remain with the principal. The law does not forbid dreaming about a new business, but it does forbid building one with the principal's resources or customer list while still employed.

The duty of loyalty appears in smaller ways as well. When Ryder, in the Scissorhands scenario, charged items knowing she lacked authorization, she violated the duty of loyalty by intentionally misleading the nursery and exposing her employer to risk. Even though the legal question there involved apparent authority, her behavior illustrated how easily the duty of loyalty can be breached when an agent prioritizes convenience or personal goals over the principal's interests.

Agent's Duties to Third Parties

Agents do not owe duties only to principals. They also

owe duties to third parties who deal with them. One major duty is the warranty of authority. When an agent enters into a contract on behalf of a principal, the agent implicitly promises that they have authority to do so. If this turns out to be false, the agent may be personally liable for the resulting damages.

The agent's liability to third parties depends heavily on whether the principal is disclosed, partially disclosed, or undisclosed. When the principal is disclosed, meaning the third party knows both that the agent is acting for a principal and who that principal is, the agent usually has no personal liability on the contract. The third party expects the principal to perform. When the principal is partially disclosed, meaning the third party knows the agent is acting for a principal but does not know the principal's identity, both the principal and the agent may be liable. When the principal is undisclosed, meaning the third party does not even know a principal exists, the agent is liable in addition to the principal. These distinctions protect third parties who bargain in good faith and rely on the identity of the other party to the contract.

For example, if a salesperson signs a contract without telling the customer that they are acting for a company, the customer may hold the salesperson personally liable. If the salesperson acts for an undisclosed principal and lacks actual authority, they also breach the warranty of authority. The law uses these doctrines to balance fairness to third parties with the realities of business practice.

In some of the nursery hypotheticals, the nursery relied entirely on Ryder's statements because it did not know her relationship with Scissorhands Landscaping. If the nursery had no reason to know she was acting for a principal, or if she claimed authority she did not have, she could be liable under these doctrines. The rules encourage agents to be transparent and to avoid overstating their authority.

Termination of Agency

An agency relationship does not last forever. It can end by agreement, by the occurrence of an event, by revocation or renunciation, or by operation of law. When the agency ends, the agent ordinarily loses all authority to act, but apparent authority may linger until third parties receive notice that the agency has ended. Termination is therefore not only a matter between the principal and agent; it also concerns those who have previously relied on the relationship.

Termination intersects with loyalty. As soon as the agency ends, the fiduciary duty of loyalty ends as well, except for obligations that naturally survive, such as the duty not to use trade secrets. This is why the employees in Foodcomm should have resigned before contacting customers for their new venture. Once an agent's relationship ends, they are free to compete, to form new partnerships, and to pursue opportunities they previously had to pass up.

Termination also matters when an agent had apparent authority. If a business fails to tell third parties that the agency has ended, those third parties may continue to rely on the agent's apparent authority. In such cases, the principal may still be bound. This is one reason many companies issue formal notices when employees leave positions where they interacted with clients or vendors. Without clear notice, the principal may be held responsible for contracts the departed agent makes after leaving.

This chapter has traced the life cycle of agency relationships, beginning with how they are formed, moving through the kinds of authority agents possess, and ending with how those relationships terminate. Agency is built on trust, control, and communication. When those elements break down, the law steps in to protect principals, agents, and third parties. As you continue your study, these themes will appear again in partnerships, LLCs, corporations, and torts. Agency law forms the foundation for understanding how people and businesses interact, how responsibility is assigned, and how the legal system tries to balance fairness with practical realities.

3 VICARIOUS LIABILITY

Vicarious liability is one of the most far-reaching doctrines in tort and agency law. It rests on an idea so simple that it almost disappears into the background of everyday business: sometimes the law holds one person responsible for the wrongful acts of another. This idea, however, carries enormous consequences. It affects the structure of businesses, the way employers train and supervise workers, and the strategies that injured plaintiffs use when seeking compensation. Vicarious liability is a doctrine that moves silently beneath the surface until something goes wrong. When an injury occurs, everything turns on the nature of the relationship between the parties.

At its core, vicarious liability is built on the concept of control. A principal or employer is responsible for the wrongful acts of an agent or employee only when the principal has the right to control the agent's actions. This requirement makes sense from both a fairness and policy standpoint. If a business directs the work of an employee, supervises the employee's activities, and benefits from the employee's labor, then the business is in the best position to prevent harm, adopt safety rules, train workers, and spread the cost of accidents. At the same time, the doctrine protects injured people by ensuring that a financially responsible party stands behind the person who caused the harm.

But while the general principle is easy to state, its application is anything but simple. Courts must distinguish between employees and independent contractors, evaluate complex franchise relationships, determine whether an agent acted within the scope of employment, and decide when joint ventures or shared-control arrangements justify imposing liability on multiple parties. Each of these questions turns on fine distinctions that can dramatically alter the outcome of a case. What follows is a thorough introduction to these central issues.

Introduction to Vicarious Liability

The traditional rule governing vicarious liability is captured by the phrase respondeat superior, meaning "let the master answer." Under this rule, an employer is liable for the torts of an employee committed within the scope of employment. This reflects a judgment that employers, as the ones directing the work, should bear the responsibility for the risks created by their business activities.

But before a court can apply respondeat superior, it must address the threshold question: was the tortfeasor an employee or an independent contractor? The classification matters because employers are typically liable for the acts of employees but not for the acts of independent contractors. Companies often attempt to classify workers as independent contractors to avoid liability, while plaintiffs argue that the worker was effectively an employee so that the employer can be held responsible.

The classification is rarely simple, and the answer often depends on a close analysis of the working relationship. As a result, cases hinge on details that might initially seem insignificant. Who supplied the equipment? Who set the schedule? Who supervised the work? Did the worker operate a business of their own, or were they integrated into the employer's operations? By asking these questions, courts can determine whether the employer exercised enough control to justify employee status.

Employee vs. Independent Contractor

Although many workers carry the title "independent contractor," courts do not take labels at face value. The true question is whether the principal had the right to control the manner and means of the worker's performance. An employer-employee relationship exists when the employer oversees how the work is done, directs the details, and treats the worker as part of the regular business. An independent contractor relationship exists when the worker maintains their own business, chooses their own methods, and operates with real independence.

Imagine a trucking company that hires drivers. If drivers own their own trucks, set their own schedules, and choose their own routes, a court might view them as independent contractors. But if the company dictates the time and place of deliveries, controls the planned route, and monitors drivers through GPS systems, the relationship may look more like employment. Similarly, a medical practice might argue that physicians working under its branding are independent contractors, but if the practice controls appointment scheduling, billing, and treatment protocols, a court might find an employment relationship.

On the other hand, consider a contractor who repairs roofs. If the roofer buys their own materials, hires assistants, negotiates their own prices, and works for multiple clients, they are likely an independent contractor. Even if a homeowner specifies when the roofer should finish the job or requires certain materials, courts usually conclude that the roofer retains enough autonomy to avoid employee status.

These distinctions matter because they determine who will bear the losses when something goes wrong. When the worker is an employee, the employer must "answer."

When the worker is an independent contractor, the principal usually escapes liability. Because so many relationships fall into gray areas, courts have developed highly fact-specific tests to evaluate control. These tests recognize that modern workers often blend features of both categories, creating classification challenges that continue to shape legal disputes.

Franchises and Apparent Agency

Franchising has transformed the modern economy. People walk into a restaurant or hotel bearing a familiar national brand and often assume that the brand owner operates the business. In reality, many of these establishments are owned by local franchisees, independent businesses licensed to use the national company's branding, products, and systems. This structure creates a difficult question for vicarious liability: should the franchisor be held liable for torts committed at a franchise location?

Courts often begin by examining control. If the franchisor controls day-to-day operations, supervises employees, or dictates how the specific instrumentality of harm is handled, then liability may follow. But franchisors typically argue that they supervise only brand standards, not daily operations. They may require a franchisee to use certain recipes, layouts, or uniforms, but they do not usually hire or supervise the workers who commit torts.

Even when franchisors avoid day-to-day control,

plaintiffs sometimes argue that the franchisor created apparent agency. Apparent agency arises when the franchisor allows the franchisee to use its branding in a way that creates the appearance of a unified enterprise. A customer staying at a hotel with a national brand's logo might reasonably believe that the national company operates the hotel. If that belief is reasonable and the injury results from reliance on that belief, a court may treat the franchisee as an apparent agent of the franchisor.

For example, if a guest selects a hotel because they trust the national brand's safety standards, and the guest later suffers an injury because the hotel failed to follow proper procedures, the guest may argue that the franchisor should be liable. Even if the franchisor did not control the particular activity that caused the harm, the branding created a reasonable belief that the franchisor stood behind the operation. Courts vary in how they apply apparent agency, but in many jurisdictions the doctrine gives plaintiffs a path to pursue the deeper pocket when the franchise structure blurs the lines of responsibility.

The tension between brand consistency and legal independence makes franchise cases both subtle and important. Franchisors wish to maintain strong brand identity without triggering liability, while plaintiffs seek to treat franchises and franchisors as a unified enterprise. The law attempts to balance these competing forces through the doctrines of control and apparent agency.

Scope of Employment

Even when the worker is clearly an employee, vicarious liability attaches only if the employee acted within the scope of employment. The scope-of-employment test reflects the idea that employers should be liable only for risks that are part of the enterprise. The key questions are whether the employee's conduct was the kind they were hired to perform, whether the conduct occurred within authorized time and space limits, and whether the conduct was at least partially motivated by a desire to serve the employer.

Consider a delivery driver who causes an accident while completing assigned deliveries. The conduct clearly falls within the scope of employment. But what if the driver stops to visit a friend or takes a detour for a personal errand? Courts analyze whether the deviation was minor or substantial. A slight detour, known as a "detour," keeps the conduct within the scope of employment. A major departure, known as a "frolic," takes the employee outside the scope and relieves the employer of liability. The line between a detour and a frolic depends on the distance, duration, and purpose of the deviation.

Intentional torts present special challenges. If an employee assaults a customer, courts must decide whether the assault was related to the employee's job. Some courts take a narrow view, concluding that intentional torts are usually driven by personal motives. But in jobs involving customer interaction, enforcement of rules, or security, courts sometimes adopt a broader view. If the job creates a foreseeable risk that an employee might act forcefully or aggressively, courts may hold the employer responsible.

Imagine a nightclub bouncer who uses excessive force to remove a patron. Even if the employer prohibited such conduct, the bouncer's job involves physical confrontation, making it more likely that the employer will be held liable. Similarly, a store manager may lose patience with an angry customer and commit a tort while trying to enforce store policies. If the confrontation arises out of the manager's duties, the employer may be responsible. Scope-of-employment cases combine legal analysis with common-sense judgments about the risks the employer's business creates.

Liability for Independent Contractors

Although principals are generally not liable for the torts of independent contractors, the rule is not absolute. Some activities are so inherently dangerous that the law imposes a non-delegable duty on the principal. Excavation, demolition, and certain forms of chemical handling often fall into this category. The idea is that some dangers are too great to shift responsibility through independent contractor arrangements. If the principal benefits from the activity, the principal must also bear its risks.

Similarly, a principal may be liable if negligent in selecting an independent contractor. If a principal hires a contractor known to be careless or unqualified, and the contractor commits a tort, the principal may be responsible for negligent hiring. The same is true when a principal retains control over part of the contractor's work. Even minimal control can create liability if the principal interferes in a way that contributes to the harm.

These exceptions remain narrow because courts wish to respect the independence of contractors and avoid turning every business relationship into a source of liability. But when the danger is great or the principal's actions contribute to the harm, courts are willing to impose liability to protect the public.

Joint Venture Liability

A joint venture is a business relationship in which two or more parties combine resources, share profits, and exercise joint control over a project or enterprise. In such cases, each participant can be held vicariously liable for the torts of the others committed in the course of the venture. This happens because each participant is treated as an agent of the others when they act within the scope of the joint undertaking.

Joint venture liability arises frequently in construction, development, and complex business collaborations. Imagine two companies that collaborate on a major building project. They share decision-making authority, divide financial risks, and coordinate operations. If an employee of one company negligently injures someone while working on the project, both companies may be liable. The key element is shared control. If one party merely invests money or provides supplies but has no control over day-to-day operations, that party is usually not a joint venturer.

Cases involving joint ventures often turn on whether the parties shared decision-making authority. Courts look to whether the parties pooled resources, participated in planning, or jointly controlled key aspects of the activity. If the evidence shows genuine collaboration, courts may impose joint liability. But if one party played only a passive or limited role, courts are reluctant to treat them as a joint venturer.

The doctrine of joint venture liability reinforces the idea that control shapes responsibility. When parties combine their influence and authority for mutual benefit, the law expects them to share responsibility for the risks they create.

Vicarious liability allocates responsibility. It reflects a balance between fairness to injured parties and fairness to businesses and individuals who may be far removed from the wrongful act. Across all of its variations — employee status, apparent agency, scope of employment, independent contractor exceptions, and joint venture liability — the doctrine emphasizes one central theme: control. The more control a principal exercises over an agent, the greater the likelihood of liability. The less control the principal has, the more the law allows the principal to avoid responsibility.

4 FORMATION, MANAGEMENT, AND CONTROL OF GENERAL PARTNERSHIPS

General partnerships are the oldest and most intuitive form of business organization. Long before the law recognized corporations or LLCs, people worked together, shared profits, divided losses, and trusted one another to act on behalf of the group. The modern law of partnerships reflects centuries of experience, capturing both the power and the peril of this simple arrangement. A partnership can be created without paperwork, without ceremony, and sometimes even without awareness. Once formed, it gives each partner enormous authority to act for the business—and exposes each partner to personal liability for the partnership's obligations. It is a structure that rewards trust and communication and punishes confusion and silence. Understanding how partnerships form, how they operate, and how they end is essential for navigating this unique blend of empowerment and risk.

Formation and the De Facto Partnership

A general partnership arises when two or more people carry on a business for profit as co-owners. This definition, elegant in its simplicity, conceals its tendency to create partnerships in unexpected places. The law does not require a written agreement, formal filings, or even the intent to form a partnership. Instead, it looks at conduct. If two people behave like partners—sharing profits, collaborating on business decisions, and presenting themselves as co-owners—the law may treat them as partners whether they wanted that result or not.

Consider the story of Meadow & Birch Landscaping, a fictional but representative example. Two neighbors, Daniel and Sofia, start doing yardwork together on weekends. At first, it is informal: they help each other with projects, borrow tools, and share ideas. But soon neighbors begin asking them to mow lawns, prune shrubs, and design garden beds. Daniel suggests that they pool the earnings to buy better equipment. Sofia agrees. They share profits evenly. They give customers a joint business card printed online. They discuss prices together and split the cost of supplies. One Saturday, a customer's tree collapses during a trimming job, damaging a fence and injuring a passerby. The insurance company denies coverage because Daniel and Sofia never bought a commercial policy. They insist they were "just helping neighbors," not running a business. But the law may see it differently. By sharing profits, making joint decisions, and presenting themselves as business co-owners, they may have formed a de facto general partnership—and each may be fully liable for the damages.

This risk also appears when people attempt to form another type of entity but do it improperly. Suppose two entrepreneurs try to create a corporation to open a bakery, Sunrise Sourdough. They draft articles of incorporation but never file them. They tell vendors they are "Sunrise Sourdough Inc." They lease space, hire staff, and place large orders for flour and equipment. They believe they have a corporation and are therefore protected from personal liability. But legally, no corporation exists. Because they are co-owners conducting a business for profit, they have inadvertently formed a partnership. Courts routinely treat improperly created corporations or LLCs as general partnerships. The consequences are severe: each partner is personally liable for all partnership debts and obligations.

The same outcome may arise when people launch an LLC but fail to file the certificate of organization or follow required formalities. Imagine two artists, Maya and Ren, who decide to sell pottery under the name Clay Collective LLC. They draft an operating agreement and order business cards. Maya believes Ren filed the required document with the state. Ren believes Maya did it. Neither does. For months they operate, taking custom orders, renting studio space, and accepting deposits. When a kiln fire damages neighboring property, their insurer discovers that Clay Collective LLC does not legally exist. Under the law, Maya and Ren may be treated as partners. Their personal assets may be at risk because they accidentally created a general partnership instead of the limited-liability entity they intended.

These examples reveal a striking truth: general partnerships arise easily and sometimes dangerously. Anyone working closely with another person to run a business must recognize that actions can carry legal implications even before intentions catch up.

Authority of Partners to Bind the Partnership

The authority structure of a general partnership is both powerful and precarious. Every partner is both an owner and an agent of the partnership. Each partner has actual authority as set out in the partnership agreement and statutory default rules. But even more importantly, each partner has apparent authority to bind the partnership in the ordinary course of business unless the partner's authority has been clearly limited and third parties have notice of those limits.

The scope of this authority often surprises new business owners. Consider a bike repair shop called PedalWorks, run by three partners: Alyssa, Brett, and Carmen. They agree informally that Alyssa handles repairs, Brett runs the front desk, and Carmen manages ordering. But they never sign a written partnership agreement. One day, Brett decides to purchase a new set of high-end tools costing thousands of dollars. He has not discussed this with Alyssa or Carmen. The vendor sees him working the front desk, reasonably believes he has the authority to buy tools, and completes the sale. When the bill arrives, Alyssa and Carmen are furious. They accuse Brett of overspending and exceeding his role. But under partnership law, Brett's actions likely bind the partnership. Purchasing tools for a bike repair shop falls squarely within the ordinary course of that business. Even if Brett lacked actual authority under their private arrangement, he possessed apparent authority. Third parties cannot be expected to know the private division of responsibilities among partners.

Another scenario shows the limits of authority. Imagine a restaurant partnership called The Golden Ladle. Three partners run it: chef-owner Lila, business manager Omar, and front-of-house coordinator Elise. The restaurant is thriving. Without consulting the others, Elise signs a contract to open a second location. She believes expansion is inevitable and wants to secure favorable rent. But opening a new location is not an ordinary-course action; it is a major strategic decision. Elise may lack both actual authority and apparent authority for such an act. If the landlord knew Elise was not a managing partner or had reason to question her power, the contract may not bind the partnership. In such cases, the law protects the partnership from unauthorized expansion that exceeds reasonable expectations.

These examples highlight the dual nature of partnership authority. It empowers each partner to act decisively, facilitating efficient operation, but it also requires partners to trust one another deeply. A single partner's decision can commit the entire business. This structure works beautifully when communication is strong and the partners share common expectations. It collapses when partners assume authority that others never intended to grant.

Partnership Agreements and Partners by Estoppel

A partnership agreement is the partners' chance to define their rights, responsibilities, management structure, profit-sharing arrangements, and procedures for disputes and dissolution. While partnerships can succeed without written agreements, doing so invites confusion and conflict. Without an agreement, statutory default rules determine everything from decision-making to profit allocation, which may not align with what the partners actually want.

Take the example of Riverbend Woodworks, a custom furniture partnership formed by three artisans: Neil, Serena, and Tomas. They agree verbally that profits will be divided based on hours worked because their contributions vary significantly. But when the business becomes profitable and disagreements arise, the absence of a written partnership agreement becomes glaring. Under default rules, partners share equally unless they have an agreement to the contrary. Because nothing is in writing, the law may treat all profits as evenly shared. The partners find themselves in conflict not because they intended unfairness, but because they failed to document their intentions.

The concept of partners by estoppel adds another layer of complexity. Sometimes, a person who is not truly a partner may be treated as one if they represent themselves as a partner or allow others to make that representation, and a third party relies on the representation. This doctrine protects business partners and third parties from misleading signals.

Imagine a family-owned bookstore called Maple & Main Booksellers. The owners, twins Jonas and Riley, run the store as partners. Their childhood friend, Sam, helps with events and promotions but is not a partner. However, Sam begins signing emails as "Partner, Maple & Main," believing it gives the store more credibility. Jonas and Riley notice but say nothing. A local printer extends credit to the store based on Sam's title. When Maple & Main falls behind on payments, the printer sues all three. Even though Sam was never formally a partner, the printer reasonably relied on Sam's representation. Sam may be treated as a partner by estoppel and held liable for the debt.

Estoppel protects the fairness and predictability of business dealings. It reminds us that representations matter and that silence can have legal consequences.

Dissociation and Dissolution: How Partnerships Change and End

Partnerships can be born easily, but they can also change

or end with equal speed. Dissociation occurs when a partner withdraws, is expelled, or otherwise ceases to be involved in management. Dissolution occurs when the partnership begins the process of winding up and terminating its affairs.

A partnership at will allows any partner to withdraw at any time. While this flexibility may be attractive, it can also introduce instability. Consider a catering partnership called Harvest Feast, run by four partners who built the business over a decade. One partner, Lena, decides she wants to pursue graduate school. She announces her dissociation. Under a partnership at will, her withdrawal triggers dissolution unless the remaining partners choose to continue the business. They scramble to decide whether to buy out her interest or liquidate the business. Their reaction illustrates how fragile partnerships can be when they rely on goodwill and ongoing commitment.

A different structure—a partnership for a definite term or particular undertaking—creates more stability. Suppose two architects form a partnership to design a specific community center. The partnership is expected to last only until the project is finished. If one architect attempts to withdraw before completion, the dissociation is wrongful. The withdrawing partner may be liable for damages, and the partnership continues until the project concludes. This structure protects the group's ability to complete significant long-term projects without fear of abrupt departures.

Dissolution itself can be orderly or chaotic. When partnerships dissolve peacefully, partners work together to complete unfinished business, pay debts, distribute remaining assets, and close the firm in good faith. But when dissolution is contentious, courts may step in. Consider a vineyard partnership in which three siblings jointly manage the land. When two want to sell and one refuses, conflicts escalate. Accusations fly about mismanagement and hidden income. Eventually, the partners seek judicial dissolution. The court evaluates whether it is practicable for them to continue working together. If not, the business may be ordered wound up and sold, with profits distributed according to partnership interests.

The process of partnership evolution—partners joining, leaving, disagreeing, or dissolving—is as human as any relationship. The law provides frameworks for fair outcomes, but it cannot erase the emotional complexity that often accompanies the end of a shared enterprise.

The Meaning of Partnership in Modern Business Life

General partnerships remain a common and powerful tool in the modern business world, even as corporations and LLCs dominate headlines. Their simplicity makes them ideal for small collaborations, professional firms, creative ventures, and emerging businesses. But their ease of creation and the personal liability they impose make them both convenient and dangerous.

The stories in this chapter illustrate that partnerships

succeed when communication is strong, expectations are clear, and mutual trust is present. They falter when assumptions replace agreements, when authority is misunderstood, or when partners fail to respect boundaries between personal and business responsibilities. The law attempts to impose fairness on these relationships, but it is ultimately the partners themselves who shape the arc of their shared enterprise.

Understanding how partnerships form, operate, and dissolve equips lawyers and non-lawyers alike to navigate one of the most human areas of business law. A partnership is, in essence, a legal way of saying: we choose to join forces, to share burdens and rewards, and to trust one another with decisions that will affect us all. The law honors that choice, supports it, and disciplines it when necessary.

5 FORMATION OF CORPORATIONS AND LIMITED LIABILITY COMPANIES

The formation of a business entity marks the moment when an idea becomes something more than a personal project—it becomes a legal person capable of owning property, entering contracts, hiring workers, and protecting its founders from personal liability. Whether entrepreneurs choose the traditional structure of a corporation or the flexible design of a limited liability company, the process of formation shapes everything that follows. Corporations rely on formal public documents, mandatory governance rules, and well-defined hierarchies, while LLCs take a freer, contract-driven approach that allows their members to design the business from the inside out. Yet both require a deliberate act of creation: filing a charter with the state, choosing a governance structure, and setting the boundaries between the business and the people who run it. Understanding how these entities are formed is the foundation for mastering the entire field of business associations.

Corporations

Corporations are everywhere in modern life, from giant tech companies shaping global markets to neighborhood coffee shops incorporated by a single owner with big dreams. Yet despite their enormous influence, corporations begin in a surprisingly humble way: with paper, signatures, and a filing fee. There is something almost magical about the moment of incorporation. An idea becomes an entity. A document becomes a legal person. A handful of words typed into a form suddenly create something that can sue, be sued, borrow, grow, fail, and outlive everyone who conceived it.

Understanding how corporations come into being requires knowing how they are built on documents—documents that sound dry but can ignite power struggles, prevent disasters, save family businesses, and give investors the confidence to trust their money to strangers. The corporate charter, the bylaws, and shareholder agreements form the backbone of corporate life. They are not exciting at first glance, but once you see what they do and how they function, they become some of the most dramatic and consequential writings in business law.

In this chapter, we explore the fundamentals of corporate governance documents. Each section includes concrete stories designed to pull you into the world of corporations and show how these documents matter not only to lawyers but also to everyday people who invest, build, and dream.

Incorporation Documents

Imagine two college friends, Maya and Luis, sitting at a kitchen table surrounded by half-empty coffee cups and a whiteboard full of ideas. They believe they've created a new kind of biodegradable packaging that could change the way small restaurants store food. They begin as many entrepreneurs do, with excitement and uncertainty. Before they can approach investors or negotiate contracts, they need a legal structure. So they decide to form a corporation.

They draft their articles of incorporation, which will become their corporation's birth certificate. In many states these articles must include the corporation's name, whether it will issue stock, the number of authorized shares, and the name of the registered agent. For Maya and Luis, choosing a corporate name seems like the simplest task, but they spend hours debating it. Names matter, not just for branding but for legal identity. Once a name is used, it becomes the label under which the corporation signs contracts, gets sued, and files taxes. They finally settle on "GreenLift Packaging Inc."

They write "GreenLift Packaging Inc." at the top of the form. With that simple action, they create an identity separate from themselves. If the business succeeds, the corporate form will protect their personal assets from business liabilities. If the business fails, creditors go after the corporation, not their homes or personal bank accounts. This protection is possible because the corporation is treated as its own legal person.

Maya and Luis add their corporate purpose. Many states allow extremely broad purposes—sometimes as broad as "to engage in any lawful activity." Other states require a specific description. They choose a broad purpose because they don't want to be trapped if the company pivots later. Right after filing, a state agency stamps their document. Just like that, their new business exists. They have not yet sold a single product, but a new legal person has been born.

This moment—filing a charter—can be deceptively simple, but it marks a powerful shift. Before incorporation, Maya and Luis were just two individuals with an idea. After incorporation, they are founders of a legal entity capable of taking risks, hiring employees, owning property, and raising capital. They have crossed from the world of individual action into the world of corporate law.

Not every corporation begins with such clarity. Sometimes people stumble into forming corporations, particularly when seeking liability protection for risky ventures. Sometimes, too, incorporation attempts fail. When that happens, courts must decide whether to treat the failed entity as a corporation anyway under doctrines like de facto corporation or corporation by estoppel. These doctrines exist to protect good-faith efforts and prevent unfair results when people act as though a corporation exists even when the paperwork is flawed. But those doctrines operate only when the parties have acted with genuine belief in their corporate status. They cannot save people who use the corporate form dishonestly.

The charter contains more than technical details. It also divides power within the corporation. It tells investors whether the corporation will issue one kind of stock or several classes with different rights. These choices determine who has voting control, who gets dividends, and who gets paid first if the company dissolves. When Maya and Luis decide to issue only one class of stock, they simplify their structure, but they also leave open the possibility of creating new classes later with different rights. Each of these choices will echo throughout the life of their corporation.

Bylaws

Filing the charter gives birth to the corporation, but the bylaws give it structure. If the charter is the corporation's skeleton, the bylaws are its muscles and circulatory system. They determine how power flows, how decisions are made, and how disputes are resolved. Without bylaws, even the simplest decisions—like scheduling the first board meeting—can become confusing.

To see why bylaws matter, imagine Maya and Luis hiring

a third founder, Priya, who brings expertise in supply-chain logistics. The three founders get along well at first, but as the business grows and pressure builds, disagreements begin. Maya wants to expand quickly by raising outside capital. Luis prefers a slower pace. Priya thinks they need to hire more engineers before expanding at all. Without clear rules about decision-making authority, these conflicts could stall the company or even destroy it.

Their bylaws step in. They explain how directors are elected, how often meetings occur, what counts as a quorum, and how many votes are needed for major decisions. They describe officer roles—CEO, CFO, secretary—and explain who has authority to sign contracts or spend money. Suddenly the disagreements have a channel. Instead of arguing endlessly, the founders follow the structure they created. If Maya, Luis, and Priya have a disagreement at the board level, the bylaws dictate how to resolve it. They may vote, consult officers, or schedule additional meetings. The corporation gains stability, not through luck but through structure.

Bylaws also carry enormous weight in litigation. When a shareholder sues the corporation, the court will examine whether meetings were held properly, votes were counted correctly, and notices were sent according to the bylaws. If officers acted without proper authorization, their actions may be invalid. In some dramatic cases, multimillion-dollar decisions have been unwound because boards failed to follow bylaw procedures.

Even small corporations depend on bylaws more than founders initially realize. Consider a husband-and-wife corporation that runs a plumbing business. At first, they operate informally and rarely look at their bylaws. But when their adult child joins the business and wants voting rights, tensions rise. The bylaws suddenly matter because they govern how new shares can be issued, how officers can be replaced, and how votes must occur. Without bylaws, the family must navigate these issues using only statutory defaults, which may not reflect their intentions.

Bylaws give corporations flexibility. Unlike charters, which require formal amendments and state filings, bylaws can change more easily. If Maya and Luis decide that monthly board meetings no longer make sense, they can amend the bylaws by board vote. If they want to redefine the CEO's authority, they can do so without filing new documents with the state. This flexibility keeps corporations adaptable as markets shift.

Amendments to Incorporation Documents and Bylaws

No corporation remains static. Markets shift, founders disagree, opportunities appear, and crises force change. Amendments allow corporations to evolve. But because amendments alter the balance of power, they can also trigger conflict, drama, and even litigation.

Changing the charter is the most serious step. It usually requires approval from both the board of directors and the shareholders. This double approval mirrors constitutional amendments in political systems. Just as a nation should not casually rewrite its founding document, a corporation should not casually rewrite its charter. When Maya and Luis's company becomes successful enough to attract venture capitalists, the investors may require charter amendments to create preferred stock with special rights. This can give investors priority in receiving dividends and sale proceeds, or give them extra voting power.

For Maya, these changes feel threatening. She fears losing control to outsiders. But for Luis, the investment represents growth they desperately need. The board debates. Lawyers prepare draft amendments. Shareholders vote. This process demonstrates how charter amendments function as a negotiation between past decisions and future plans. Once approved, these amendments reshape the corporate power structure in fundamental ways.

Amending bylaws can be equally dramatic, though usually easier. Sometimes boards amend bylaws to defend against unwanted takeovers. A determined investor might try to accumulate shares quietly and then take control. The board, seeking to protect the corporation, might amend the bylaws to require longer notice periods for meetings or increase quorum requirements. These tactics, often called "poison pills" or "defensive amendments," show how bylaws are not merely technical documents but strategic tools.

In family corporations, amendments can be emotional. Imagine a family-owned bakery whose bylaws allocate one board seat to each parent. When the parents retire and want to give their daughter full authority, they must amend the bylaws to redefine director roles. If the son disagrees, the amendment process becomes a battleground for family identity and legacy.

Amendments also occur when corporations face crisis. If a key officer disappears or dies, bylaws may need updating. If a corporation shifts from manufacturing goods to providing digital services, the charter may need new purpose language. These changes allow corporations to adapt while maintaining their identity.

Shareholder Agreements

If the charter is the constitution and the bylaws are the instruction manual, shareholder agreements are private treaties among the people who actually own the corporation. They are especially important in small or closely held corporations, where shareholders have personal relationships and want to preserve harmony, stability, or control over the future.

Imagine three siblings—Alex, Jamie, and Taylor—who inherit a small construction company from their parents. Each owns one-third of the shares. Alex wants to expand aggressively. Jamie wants to maintain the traditional, steady approach. Taylor wants to convert part of the business into renewable energy contracting. Without a shareholder agreement, disagreements among them could paralyze the company. A shareholder agreement can prevent this by spelling out how conflicts are resolved, how voting rights work, and what happens if one sibling wants to sell their shares.

One common provision in shareholder agreements is the buy-sell clause. Suppose Taylor wants to leave the business. Without restrictions, Taylor could sell their shares to anyone—from a local competitor to an ex-spouse. A buy-sell agreement requires Taylor to offer the shares first to Alex and Jamie, then to the corporation itself, before selling to outsiders. This protects the business from unwanted ownership changes.

Another example comes from start-up companies. Picture four founders in a software company. They share a vision and work equally hard in the early months. But one of them, Sam, leaves within a year to take a job elsewhere. Without a shareholder agreement, Sam might keep one-quarter of the company forever, benefiting from the hard work of the remaining founders. A shareholder agreement can include a vesting schedule, which cancels or repurchases shares held by early departing founders. This ensures fairness and keeps ownership aligned with contribution.

Shareholder agreements can also address voting arrangements. Imagine an investor who buys twenty percent of Maya and Luis's corporation. The founders worry that this investor may form alliances with others to take control. A shareholder agreement could require unanimous approval for certain major decisions, such as selling the company or dissolving it. These agreements offer stability and predictability in moments of uncertainty.

Of course, shareholder agreements have limits. They cannot override mandatory corporate law or eliminate essential director powers. Courts will not enforce agreements that cripple the board or prevent it from acting in the corporation's interest. But within these limits, shareholder agreements provide a rich field for creativity and negotiation.

Thus, corporations may begin with documents, but those documents shape human stories—stories of trust, conflict, ambition, compromise, and sometimes heartbreak. Incorporation forms the foundation. Bylaws guide internal operations. Amendments allow evolution. Shareholder agreements protect relationships and expectations. Each document plays a different role, but together they create a system that allows strangers to collaborate, investors to trust, and businesses to grow beyond the limits of a single lifetime.

Limited Liability Companies

If the corporation is the grand old institution of American business law, the limited liability company—usually called the LLC—is the rebellious younger sibling who saw how corporations were run and decided to do things differently. In just a few decades, LLCs have risen from an experimental idea to one of the most dominant business forms in the country. Small businesses use them, family investors use them, artists use them, and many startups begin life as LLCs before converting into corporations later. Even sophisticated investment funds and real estate holdings choose LLC structures because of the freedom they offer.

To truly understand LLCs, it helps to compare them to the corporate world that dominated business law for so long. Corporations are structured, predictable, and rule-bound. They rely on charters, bylaws, boards of directors, officers, and shareholder votes. LLCs—by contrast—are built around flexibility. They allow their members to define their own rules, their own processes, and their own power structures. While corporations run on a familiar hierarchy, LLCs run on private ordering and contractual freedom.

This chapter explores the three pillars of LLC formation and governance: the certificate of organization, the operating agreement, and the amendment process. To bring these concepts to life, the chapter uses vivid examples and comparisons to corporations, so you can see how LLCs work in practice and how they differ from their more rigid corporate cousins.

Certificate of Organization

Every LLC begins with a document filed with the state. Depending on the jurisdiction, this document might be called the certificate of organization, certificate of formation, the articles of organization, or something similar. Although the vocabulary changes from state to state, the purpose remains constant: this certificate is the LLC's birth certificate, similar to how the articles of incorporation bring a corporation into existence. But while the corporate charter is thick with long-term, non-negotiable rules, the LLC certificate is usually simple and restrained—a skeleton waiting for flesh.

To understand this difference, imagine two entrepreneurs, Daniel and Nina, who want to open a craft brewery. If they form a corporation, the articles of incorporation must contain fairly specific information: the classes of shares, the number of authorized shares, the name and address of the registered agent, the identity of the incorporators, and sometimes the purpose of the corporation. These choices can have major consequences down the road, shaping ownership and control.

Now imagine Daniel and Nina choose instead to form an LLC. They download a certificate of organization form from the state's website. To their surprise, the form is short—shockingly short compared to the corporate version. It usually requires only the LLC's name, its registered agent, and sometimes whether it will be managed by members or by managers. In some states, even the management structure doesn't have to be disclosed. Instead of six or seven pages, the certificate of organization may fit on a single sheet of paper. Daniel laughs when he realizes he can fill out the entire form in less time than it takes to brew a single cup of coffee.

This simplicity reflects a deep philosophical difference. Corporations depend on public-facing documents because investors rely on formal structures and legally mandated protections. LLCs depend on private agreements among their members, which the law respects even when they deviate sharply from traditional rules. Where corporations declare their structure publicly in their charters, LLCs hide their internal mechanics behind a minimalist certificate and push the real governance decisions into the operating agreement. In essence, the certificate of organization says, "We exist," and the operating agreement says, "Here is how we choose to exist."

Despite its simplicity, the certificate of organization is still essential. It creates the legal entity. It separates the founders' personal assets from the liabilities of the business. Once it is filed and accepted, the LLC becomes a legal person, capable of owning land, opening bank accounts, entering contracts, and protecting its members from personal responsibility for business debts. This limited liability is the beating heart of both corporations and LLCs—but the similarity ends there. The paths diverge dramatically once we turn to the operating agreement.

Operating Agreement

If corporate law centers on charters and bylaws, LLC law centers overwhelmingly on the operating agreement. This document—or sometimes unwritten agreement, since many states permit oral or implied operating agreements—controls almost everything about how the LLC functions. It defines who has power, who shares profits, who makes decisions, and what happens when the unexpected occurs.

Imagine Daniel and Nina drafting their LLC's operating agreement. They sit across from each other at a brewery table, stacks of sample agreements spread around them. Daniel wants equal voting power. Nina wants decisions about marketing to require unanimous approval because brand identity is incredibly important to her. They debate how much authority to give the manager they plan to hire. They discuss what happens if one of them becomes disabled or wants to sell their ownership stake. These discussions feel personal, almost intimate, because the operating agreement is not just a governance document—it is a contract grounded in trust, prediction, and sometimes fear.

Comparing corporations and LLCs reveals how startlingly different their governance structures can be. In a corporation, shareholders elect a board, the board appoints officers, and the officers run the business. This hierarchy is not optional. Even if a corporation wanted to abolish its board and operate by consensus, the law would not allow it. The corporate structure is mandatory. LLCs reject this rigidity entirely. Members can run the business directly in a member-managed LLC, or they can appoint managers in a manager-managed LLC. They can create hybrid structures with committees, rotating leadership, or special veto rights. They can distribute profits in any manner they choose, without regard to ownership percentages. They can design voting rights to be equal, weighted, or conditional.

This freedom allows LLCs to fit any number of human relationships. For example, consider a three-person film production group—Jordan, Alex, and Kai. Jordan is the creative force behind the project. Alex handles financing. Kai manages day-to-day logistics. In a corporation, all three might get identical shares unless they design complicated stock classes. In an LLC, their operating agreement can divide profits however they wish: perhaps 40 percent to Jordan, 40 percent to Alex, and 20 percent to Kai. Or maybe Jordan receives a special priority return until production costs are recovered. These possibilities are limited mainly by imagination, not by statute.

Operating agreements also allow LLCs to plan for real-world challenges. What happens if a member wants to withdraw? What if the company needs additional capital? What if a member dies or divorces? Corporations address these questions indirectly, usually through default statutory rules or shareholder agreements. LLCs address them directly through the operating agreement. Because the agreement functions as a contract, courts generally enforce its terms strictly, even when those terms depart from corporate norms.

Some states even recognize implied operating agreements—agreements formed through the conduct of the members rather than a written document. Imagine two friends, Sam and Riley, who start an LLC to renovate houses. They never sign an operating agreement but act as though they are equal partners, make all major decisions together, and share profits fifty-fifty. A court may determine that they formed an implied operating agreement through their behavior. This feature of LLC law reflects its roots in contract theory: what the parties actually agreed to—whether orally, in writing, or through conduct—controls.

This flexibility is powerful, but it can be dangerous. When LLC members fail to communicate clearly or neglect to draft a written agreement, ambiguities can lead to costly disputes. Courts sometimes must decide who has authority, who owns what, or how profits should be divided. A corporation's rigidity, in such moments, can feel like a blessing. But for well-advised and well-organized LLC members, the freedom of the operating agreement allows the business to reflect human relationships far more accurately than the corporate structure ever could.

Amendments to Certificate of Organization and Operating Agreement

No business plan survives first contact with reality. Markets shift. People change. New opportunities appear. Conflicts emerge. For LLCs, the amendment process allows the business to evolve without being trapped by earlier decisions.

Changing the certificate of organization is usually straightforward. Because the document is short and formal, amendments typically involve only basic information: updating the registered agent, changing the LLC's name, or altering whether the LLC is member-managed or manager-managed. These amendments resemble corporate charter amendments in that they must be filed with the state. But unlike corporate amendments, LLC amendments rarely affect power dynamics or ownership rights. They operate more like reporting updates than structural changes.

The operating agreement, however, is where amendment drama often unfolds. Imagine Daniel and Nina's brewery five years later. The business is thriving. They have opened two locations, hired more staff, and attracted an investor named Layla who contributes a substantial amount of capital. Because Layla's contribution dwarfs the founders' initial investments, she wants a larger share of profits and a say in major decisions. Daniel and Nina, grateful for the infusion of money but protective of their vision, must decide whether to amend the operating agreement to give Layla voting rights, profit rights, or veto powers.

These negotiations can feel tense. The operating agreement is the DNA of the LLC, and altering it can feel like rewriting the company's identity. Unlike corporations—where voting rules for charter amendments are usually dictated by statute—LLCs can set their own amendment procedures. Some require unanimous consent. Some require a majority. Some specify that certain members have veto rights. If the operating agreement is silent, default statutory rules apply, which may or may not reflect the members' expectations.

Consider another hypothetical. A four-member real estate LLC buys apartment buildings and divides profits equally. Over time, two members—Carla and Dev—spend far more time managing the properties than the others. They propose amending the operating agreement to grant them larger profit shares and additional voting rights. But the original agreement requires unanimous approval for amendments. The other two members refuse, creating deadlock. In a corporation, this kind of conflict would usually follow formal voting and statutory procedures. In an LLC, the private agreement rules everything. If the operating agreement requires unanimity, there is no legal mechanism to force change, even when the original structure becomes unfair or impractical.

This combination of flexibility and vulnerability makes LLC amendments a double-edged sword. When members communicate well, amendment processes allow LLCs to adapt gracefully to new realities. When relationships sour, the amendment process can freeze the business in outdated structures, sometimes pushing members to seek judicial dissolution or forced buyouts.

Through all of this, the contrast with corporations

remains sharp. Corporations prioritize stability and predictability. LLCs prioritize freedom and private ordering. The amendment processes reflect those values. For corporations, amendments feel like constitutional revisions. For LLCs, amendments feel like renegotiating a contract—sometimes constructive, sometimes contentious, but always rooted in the expectations and dynamics of the members themselves.

Conclusion

LLCs offer a new way of imagining business relationships. Where corporations rely on strict hierarchy, LLCs embrace flexibility. Where corporations depend on public documents, LLCs depend on private agreements. Where corporations constrain private ordering through mandatory rules, LLCs express it through contractual freedom.

The certificate of organization is the quiet beginning—a small, minimal document that signals the LLC's existence but reveals almost nothing about how it will function. The operating agreement is the heart, the brain, and the soul of the entity, shaping relationships, allocations, voting rights, and future plans. And the amendment process reflects the LLC's essential character: adaptable, customizable, and deeply dependent on cooperation.

Understanding LLCs through the lens of corporations illuminates both structures more clearly. Corporations are designed for large-scale investment, passive shareholders, and standardized roles. LLCs are designed for flexibility, closely held ownership, and individualized bargaining. Each form carries strengths and weaknesses. The corporate form shines in clarity and predictability. The LLC thrives on freedom and adaptability.

As you continue through your study of business associations, you will see these contrasts again and again—in fiduciary duties, in litigation rights, in dissolution rules, and in the way each business form responds to conflict. For now, remember that LLCs are not simply "corporations with different paperwork." They represent a fundamentally different philosophy of business law, one that values the private choices of the members above the rigid frameworks of tradition.

6 CORPORATE PROMOTERS: BUILDING CORPORATIONS BEFORE THEY EXIST

Every corporation has a beginning, and that beginning is almost never as clean or tidy as the formation documents suggest. Before the articles of incorporation are filed, before bylaws are drafted, before the corporation has a bank account or a name, someone has to act. Someone has to find investors, negotiate leases, secure equipment, hire employees, buy inventory, or scout opportunities. That someone is the promoter. Promoters occupy a strange position in corporate law. They act for a business that does not yet exist, on behalf of people who may not yet be shareholders, in pursuit of goals that may change as the corporation forms. They are dreamers, planners, negotiators, and sometimes gamblers. Some are founders who will eventually run the corporation. Others are intermediaries whose role ends at formation. In every case, promoters create the runway that allows a corporation to take off. But with this power comes legal complexity. Promoters act before the corporation exists, and because a non-existent entity cannot sign contracts, the law must make decisions about who is bound by the agreements promoters enter. Promoters may find themselves personally liable, even if they intended the future corporation to shoulder the burden. They may owe fiduciary duties to the to-be-formed corporation, even though that corporation does not yet exist. They must also navigate the process by which the newly formed corporation can adopt, ratify, or reject the promoter's contracts. Understanding promoters is like watching the backstage workers in a theater production. The audience sees the final show, but the promoter moves the scenery, hires the actors, negotiates with the venue, and orders costumes long before opening night. If something goes wrong at this early stage—if they overpromise, mislead, or mishandle funds—the entire production can collapse before a single ticket is sold. What follows is a deep exploration of promoters, told through narrative, hypothetical scenarios, and comparisons to familiar contract-law doctrines. This chapter aims to bring clarity and life to a topic that often appears abstract but is rooted in the very real challenges of starting a business.

The Role of the Promoter

Imagine two engineers, Harper and Miguel, who dream of launching a renewable-energy design company. They want to sell compact solar units for rural homes. They talk late into the night, bundled over schematics and sketches, imagining how many households they could reach. They know they want to form a corporation eventually, but that step requires time and legal fees. Meanwhile, opportunity is knocking. A regional utility company is interested in partnering. A manufacturer in Taiwan is willing to produce the units. A warehouse space is available at a price that will not last. Harper and Miguel begin acting as promoters. They call suppliers, negotiate pricing, and even draft a preliminary agreement with the manufacturer. They sign this agreement as "Harper and Miguel, on behalf of SolarNest Inc.," even though SolarNest Inc. does not yet exist. To the manufacturer, this uncertainty may be unimportant. They trust the relationship. But the law cares deeply. A business that does not exist cannot enter into a contract, and so the question becomes: who has actually agreed to the deal? The future corporation? Harper and Miguel? Some hybrid of the two? In many cases, the law treats promoters as personally liable because the corporation cannot be liable for something done before it existed. This is both intuitive and counterintuitive. On the one hand, the corporation cannot bear burdens before it exists, just as a person cannot be bound by promises made before they are born. On the other hand, promoters often act solely for the benefit of the future corporation and do not intend to take on personal liability. They are merely the bridge between idea and entity. These tensions give rise to the doctrine of promoter liability.

Personal Liability of Promoters

Returning to Harper and Miguel's situation, imagine the manufacturer ships an initial trial batch of solar units before the corporation is formed. Before shipment arrives, Harper and Miguel learn that the warehouse rental fell through, and they can't afford a new space. When the manufacturer demands payment, the corporation still does not exist. The manufacturer sues. The manufacturer cannot sue SolarNest Inc., because that company does not yet exist. So the manufacturer sues Harper and Miguel personally. The law typically allows this because promoters are generally personally liable on pre-incorporation contracts unless the contract explicitly shows that the third party agreed to look solely to the future corporation. In most real situations, third parties want assurance that someone—whether the promoter or the future corporation—will pay. If the promoter wants to avoid liability, the contract must clearly state that the third party agrees not to hold the promoter personally liable. Courts sometimes frame promoter liability as a matter of agency. A person cannot be an agent for a nonexistent principal. Because the corporation does not yet exist, the promoter cannot bind it. The promoter therefore binds only themselves. This may feel unfair to promoters who acted in good faith. But the rule protects third parties from promises made on behalf of imaginary entities that cannot be sued. Now imagine another variation. Suppose Harper and Miguel include a line in the contract stating: "The manufacturer agrees to look solely to the corporation once formed for its payment obligations." This language helps, but even then, many courts hold that promoters remain liable unless the contract clearly releases them. The law dislikes gaps in liability. It wants a responsible party. Promoters may escape liability only if all parties agree, explicitly and unequivocally, that the promoter is off the hook. These rules push promoters to be careful and transparent. If promoters want to avoid personal liability, they must negotiate releases, disclaimers, or special terms upfront. They cannot assume that the corporation's future formation will rescue them. If the corporation is never formed, or if it declines to adopt the contract, the promoter remains the debtor.

Fiduciary Duties of Promoters

Promoters do not merely negotiate contracts; they also owe fiduciary duties to the future corporation. This duty arises from the trust involved. Promoters often handle money, property, or opportunities intended for the corporation. They act as architects of the future business, and as such, they must not use the position for personal advantage at the corporation's expense. To see how this plays out, imagine Harper discovers a vacant warehouse perfect for SolarNest's operations. Instead of securing it for the future corporation, Harper quietly signs a personal lease and then proposes that the corporation, once formed, sublease from Harper at a higher price. Harper rationalizes this by thinking, "I found the opportunity; I should benefit." But the law sees this as a breach of fiduciary duty. Promoters must disclose personal interests and cannot profit secretly from transactions involving the to-be-formed corporation. Courts often treat promoters similarly to agents or trustees. They must act in good faith, avoid conflicts of interest, disclose material information, and refrain from usurping corporate opportunities. Even though the corporation does not yet exist, courts treat it as a future beneficiary whose interests must be protected. Another example highlights this duty even more sharply. Suppose Miguel negotiates with a manufacturer and secures a low price for the solar units. Instead of passing those savings on to the future corporation, Miguel forms a separate LLC, buys the units at the low price, and then sells them to the corporation at a markup. Courts would likely treat this as self-dealing. Even though the future corporation is not yet alive, the promoter cannot position themselves to profit unfairly from its formation. These duties protect future shareholders and prevent promoters from creating corporations that begin life burdened by lopsided obligations or compromised opportunities. The law wants corporations to be born clean, not tarnished by hidden deals or promoter conflicts.

Adoption and Ratification of Pre-Organization Contracts

Once a corporation is formed, it can decide whether to adopt the contracts its promoters entered. Adoption and ratification are often discussed together, but they operate differently. Adoption occurs when the corporation, after coming into existence, accepts the benefits of a pre-incorporation contract or formally agrees to be bound by its terms. Adoption does not erase promoter liability. It simply adds the corporation as a liable party. Imagine SolarNest Inc. is finally formed. The new board reviews the manufacturer contract and likes it. They vote to adopt the agreement. The manufacturer can now sue the corporation. But the promoter—Harper and Miguel—also remain liable unless the manufacturer releases them. The adoption creates a second liable party; it does not erase the first. Ratification, however, is trickier. Technically, only an existing principal can ratify an act. Because the corporation did not exist at the time of the promoter's contract, true ratification is impossible. Some courts blur this distinction and treat adoption as ratification for practical purposes, but the traditional rule remains that promoters remain liable even if the corporation "ratifies" their agreements. The key takeaway is that only a novation—discussed later—can fully release a promoter from liability. Promoters often assume that once the corporation adopts their contract, their personal liability disappears. This misunderstanding has trapped many founders. Adoption is not release; it is acceptance. The corporation steps into the shoes of a co-obligor, not a replacement. To relieve the promoter of liability, the corporation and the third party must enter into a novation.

Assignment and Assumption

Assignment and assumption are additional ways the newly formed corporation can take on a promoter's contract. Assignment occurs when the promoter transfers their rights under the contract to the corporation. Assumption occurs when the corporation takes on the duties. Third parties must generally agree to assumption because it alters their expectations about who is performing the contractual obligations. Imagine Harper signs a supply contract with a manufacturer that includes a clause requiring personal performance or personal oversight. Harper cannot simply assign the contract to SolarNest Inc. without the manufacturer's consent. Even where the contract is assignable, the assumption of duties by the corporation does not remove Harper from liability unless the third party agrees to release them. Assignment and assumption therefore function similarly to adoption: they may bring the corporation into the contract, but they do not expel the promoter from it. This reflects a broader principle in contract law: parties cannot force substitutions onto an unwilling counterparty. A person cannot agree with themselves to be replaced. The manufacturer must agree to treat the corporation as the new obligor. If they do not agree, the promoter remains liable.

Novation and Other Contract Discharge Doctrines

The only mechanism that fully releases a promoter from personal liability is novation. A novation is a new contract that replaces the promoter with the corporation, extinguishing the old contract and substituting a new obligor. It requires agreement by all three parties: the promoter, the corporation, and the third party. Imagine SolarNest Inc. becomes profitable and the board wants to clean up early liabilities. They approach the manufacturer and propose a novation: the corporation will take over the contract entirely, and the manufacturer will release Harper and Miguel. The manufacturer, seeing the corporation as more stable and better funded, agrees. Only now are Harper and Miguel fully free. Novation differs from related doctrines. A substituted contract replaces the old one but does not necessarily change the obligor. A rescission cancels the contract entirely. A release allows one party to waive claims. These doctrines may appear in promoter situations, but only novation specifically allows the corporation to replace the promoter. The connection to contract law emphasizes how promoters live in the liminal space between formation and existence, making agreements in a legal no-man's land. Without careful drafting and negotiation, promoters may unintentionally bind themselves in ways they never intended.

Putting It All Together: A Complete Narrative

To understand how these doctrines intersect, imagine the full lifecycle of SolarNest's formation. Harper and Miguel negotiate with suppliers, secure preliminary agreements, and hire a graphic designer to create a brand identity. They sign these contracts as promoters. They assume, perhaps naïvely, that the future corporation will shoulder all liabilities. They act in good faith, but they do not consult legal counsel. They also do not disclose that Harper signed a warehouse lease under his own name with the intent of leasing it to the corporation at a markup. When SolarNest Inc. is finally formed, the board discovers Harper's self-dealing. They accuse him of breaching fiduciary duties. The manufacturer demands payment for the trial batch of solar units. The graphic designer invoices for the branding materials and wants payment immediately. Harper and Miguel find themselves personally liable on all these contracts because the corporation had not yet adopted them and third parties had not executed novations. The new board adopts the manufacturer contract but not the warehouse lease. Adoption makes SolarNest liable, but Harper and Miguel remain personally liable unless the manufacturer agrees to release them. They request a novation, and after tense negotiation, the manufacturer accepts. Harper is forced to unwind the warehouse lease, make restitution for his attempted markup, and apologize formally to the board. The board updates internal policies for how pre-formation activities must be handled in the future. The messy birth of SolarNest illustrates why promoter law matters. Promoters often operate in uncertainty, driven by opportunity and momentum, but the law insists on clarity, disclosure, and fairness. Promoters who understand their duties and liabilities can navigate formation wisely. Those who do not can find themselves personally entangled in obligations they never intended to bear.

In conclusion, promoters are the bridge between dream and corporation. They negotiate, plan, and assemble the foundation on which the business will stand. But they operate in a legally hazardous landscape where the corporation does not yet exist to shield them or validate their actions. The law imposes personal liability unless contracts clearly release them, fiduciary duties to prevent misuse of power, and procedural requirements for transferring obligations to the newly formed corporation. Understanding promoters is essential for grasping the deeper logic of corporate formation. It reveals how law protects future shareholders, how contracts function across temporal gaps, and how early decisions shape a corporation long after its birth. Promoters carry great power, and with it, great vulnerability. Their choices—whether transparent or self-interested, careful or careless—set the tone for the future corporation. When promoters act with care, corporations begin life on solid ground. When they act with haste or self-interest, the consequences may follow the corporation for years. Promoters stand at the threshold of corporate existence, shaping what the corporation will become before it draws its first legal breath. Understanding their role is the key to understanding corporate birth itself.

7 MANAGEMENT AND CONTROL OF CORPORATIONS AND LIMITED LIABILITY COMPANIES

Management is the beating heart of any business entity. It determines who makes decisions, who carries responsibility, who exercises power, and who ultimately shapes the fate of the enterprise. Some entities operate with strict hierarchy, where authority flows downward with clear rules and expectations. Others choose fluid structures, where power is shared or customized by agreement. Corporations and limited liability companies represent two very different visions of organizational control: one built on tradition, predictability, and well-worn governance procedures, and the other built on flexibility, contractual freedom, and adaptability.

Understanding management and control is essential to understanding business entities themselves. A corporation can raise mountains of capital, but a confused or divided board can bring it crashing down. An LLC can adapt beautifully to the relationships of its members, but an unclear or poorly drafted operating agreement can paralyze decision-making. This chapter explores these themes by comparing and contrasting the roles of those who run corporations—shareholders, directors, and officers—with the powers held by LLC members and managers. Through narrative examples and practical illustrations, the goal is to bring these structures to life, showing why management rules matter not just in statutes, but in the day-to-day drama of running a business.

Corporations

Corporations divide power among three groups: shareholders, directors, and officers. Each plays a distinct role in the governance ecosystem. Shareholders own the corporation but do not run it. Directors run the corporation but do so collectively, supervising and directing the business at a strategic level. Officers handle daily operations, carrying out the policies that the board approves.

This separation is deliberate. Corporations often have many shareholders, sometimes thousands or even millions. If ownership and management overlapped too heavily, chaos would follow. Instead, the law builds a structure where shareholders provide capital, directors provide oversight, and officers provide execution. Each group has powers, rights, and responsibilities shaped by both statute and common law.

Powers and Rights of Shareholders

Shareholders occupy a curious position. They own the corporation, yet they do not manage it. Their power is real but episodic, exercised mostly through voting. Their votes elect directors, approve mergers, and shape the fundamental structure of the corporation.

Consider the case of Brent, a young engineer who buys shares in a robotics startup called ApexMotion Corporation. Brent believes in its technology but has no interest in managing the business himself. Months later, he receives notice of the annual meeting. The notice lists candidates for the board, including the charismatic founder who wants to expand aggressively and a more cautious candidate favored by institutional investors. Although Brent cannot dictate strategy directly, his vote influences the company's direction. He sits at his laptop in a quiet apartment, clicks a few boxes, and casts his proxy. That single vote joins millions of others to choose who will guide ApexMotion.

The annual meeting is not merely a formality. It is the primary arena where shareholder democracy unfolds. Some meetings unfold quietly; others resemble political battles. In one famous proxy fight in a different company, a small activist hedge fund traveled the country giving presentations in hotel ballrooms, trying to convince ordinary shareholders that the board had grown complacent. Battles like these can reshape entire industries.

Shareholders may act without meetings through written consents. Imagine a family-owned corporation with only four shareholders—all sisters who inherited a chain of bakeries. They rarely hold formal meetings. Instead, they sign written consents around the kitchen table, approving decisions between bites of pie.

Shareholders can hold different classes of stock. Preferred shareholders may receive guaranteed dividends. Common shareholders may have greater voting power. These differences matter when corporations face financial difficulty. Suppose a biotech startup fails a critical trial. Preferred shareholders may still receive liquidation preferences if the company sells its remaining assets, while common shareholders receive nothing. The structure of shares affects both control and financial consequences.

Preemptive rights allow shareholders to maintain their percentage ownership. For example, a brewery called IronWheel Corp. wants to expand by issuing 500,000 new shares. Elaine, an early investor, fears losing voting power. Preemptive rights give her a chance to buy additional shares first. If she chooses not to, the corporation can sell them to others. This mechanic preserves fairness for long-term investors.

Watered stock illustrates a different problem. Suppose directors issue stock to themselves for far less than its fair value, hiding the transaction from the public. Creditors later discover the deception and sue. Those directors can be held responsible for the "water" in the stock. While modern corporate statutes reduce these cases, they still teach an important lesson: corporate governance must be transparent and honest.

Through these examples, shareholder power comes into sharper focus. Shareholders cannot run the business day-to-day, but their votes influence its direction, their rights guard its fairness, and their powers provide the democratic foundation on which corporations rest.

Powers and Rights of Directors

If shareholders are the owners, directors are the strategists and guardians. Directors make major decisions: approving mergers, setting policies, selecting officers, declaring dividends, and charting the corporation's long-term vision.

Imagine ApexMotion Corp.'s board meeting in a high-rise overlooking the city. Twelve directors gather around a long table. Some are venture capitalists who funded the company years earlier; some are independent directors with experience in robotics, supply chains, or ethics. The CEO presents a proposal to acquire a small AI research lab. The CFO warns that the price may strain the company's budget. The board debates. A director who once ran her own robotics company raises concerns about integration challenges. After discussion, they vote. Their decision influences the future of every employee, every shareholder, and every customer.

Director meetings require notice and quorum to ensure fairness. Notice gives directors time to prepare; quorum ensures that decisions represent the board's collective judgment. Directors cannot simply whisper in a hallway and decide the corporation's fate.

Sometimes boards meet by video conference. Picture directors scattered across the globe: one in Singapore drinking morning tea, another in Berlin at sunset, and a third in San Francisco finishing lunch. They dial into a secure video call. As long as they can hear each other, the meeting is valid.

Committees play a crucial role. Audit committees oversee financial integrity. Compensation committees evaluate executive pay—which can be controversial. Imagine a committee wrestling with whether to approve a $50 million stock package for the CEO. Some directors argue it attracts top talent; others fear it will anger investors. The committee's decision shapes corporate culture and public perception.

Staggered boards add another layer. In a staggered board, only a portion of directors are elected each year. This makes hostile takeovers harder. In one real-world example, a struggling retail chain survived a takeover attempt because its staggered board prevented rapid replacement of directors. That extra time allowed the company to reorganize, eventually returning to profitability.

Indemnification protects directors from personal ruin. Imagine a director sued after the corporation suffers a data breach. She acted responsibly, relying on expert advice, yet a shareholder lawsuit includes her name. Indemnification and D&O insurance allow her to defend herself without risking her home or retirement savings. Without these protections, corporations might struggle to find qualified directors willing to accept the risks.

Cumulative voting introduces another narrative thread. Imagine a minority shareholder—perhaps Brent in ApexMotion—disagrees strongly with the board's direction. Through cumulative voting, he and other small investors pool their voting power to elect one director sympathetic to their concerns. That single director becomes the voice of minority shareholders in a room otherwise dominated by institutional investors. In one well-known corporation, a minority-supported director became the crucial vote that halted a risky acquisition and saved the company from bankruptcy.

Directors operate in the high-altitude world of strategy and oversight. Their decisions can change industries. Their debates can determine whether corporations sink or soar.

Powers and Rights of Officers

If directors operate in the boardroom, officers operate everywhere else—factories, warehouses, offices, and online spaces. They are the hands and feet of the corporation.

Imagine ApexMotion's CEO, Priya, who starts her day at 5 a.m. reviewing reports about a supply chain delay caused by flooding in Malaysia. She spends the morning negotiating with alternative suppliers. At noon, she meets with engineers to approve a design change. In the afternoon, she speaks with investors in a video conference. In the evening, she prepares a presentation for the next board meeting. Priya's authority flows from the board, but her decisions ripple through every corner of the corporation.

Officers can bind the corporation contractually. If Priya signs a contract within her scope of authority, the corporation is liable. But if she leaps beyond her role, problems arise. Imagine Priya's chief marketing officer decides, without approval, to sign a multi-year lease for a new headquarters. If this falls outside her authority, the board may refuse to honor the contract. The landlord may argue apparent authority: "She was a high-ranking officer. I reasonably believed she could sign." Such disputes can lead to litigation.

Officers represent the corporation, and in moments of crisis, their leadership matters tremendously. Consider a public relations nightmare—a product malfunction injures several consumers. The CFO must assess financial exposure. The general counsel must evaluate liability and contact regulators. The CEO must speak publicly with clarity and empathy. Directors supervise, but officers act immediately. Their judgment under pressure can save or destroy corporate reputation.

Officers' personal liability also arises when they sign contracts without clarifying that they act on behalf of the corporation. Imagine a rushed moment: the chief operating officer signs a supply contract but forgets to add the corporation's name beneath his signature. If the supplier later suffers losses, it may sue him personally. Such small errors can have enormous consequences.

Officers stand at the crossroads of authority and execution. Their decisions make the corporate machinery run—or stall.

Powers and Rights of Members and Managers of Limited Liability Companies

LLCs represent a different philosophy. They favor flexibility, customization, and contractual freedom. Members can choose how to manage the company: collectively, through designated managers, or through a hybrid model.

Consider a member-managed LLC. Three friends—Jake, Milena, and Oscar—open a farm-to-table restaurant. They operate as a member-managed LLC because they trust each other and want equal power. Jake manages suppliers. Milena handles marketing. Oscar runs day-to-day operations. When Jake orders produce, his signature binds the LLC. When Oscar hires a sous chef, the contract binds the LLC. Their authority is mutual and automatic unless limited by the operating agreement.

But personal relationships, like businesses, evolve. After

two years, Oscar becomes overwhelmed. Milena wants a more structured approach. They amend the operating agreement to create a manager-managed LLC, appointing Milena the sole manager. Jake and Oscar remain members with voting rights on major decisions. Milena now signs contracts, supervises staff, and manages suppliers. If Oscar tries to sign a catering contract with a wedding venue, the venue must verify whether he has authority. If not, the LLC may refuse the contract.

Manager-managed LLCs often arise when founders bring in passive investors. Suppose Milena wants to expand the restaurant into a franchise. She needs capital and approaches investors who want profits but not daily involvement. They contribute funds and gain membership interests, but Milena remains the manager. Their operating agreement specifies voting rights, veto powers, and distribution rules tailored to the investors' expectations.

LLCs allow remarkable customization. Members can adjust quorum rules, set supermajority voting for major decisions, or assign unique powers to particular individuals. Imagine an LLC formed by four artists running a studio. They tailor the operating agreement to protect their creative values: a supermajority vote is required before accepting commercial commissions. This prevents large corporations from steering the studio's artistic direction.

In another example, a family-owned real estate LLC

names the aging parent as "senior manager," giving her authority to approve all property sales for as long as she chooses. This arrangement might be impossible in a corporation but works in an LLC due to contractual freedom.

LLCs can operate informally, sometimes too informally. In one case, a four-member LLC never wrote an operating agreement. They ran a craft brewery based on trust and conversation. When a disagreement arose about expanding production, the absence of a written agreement caused chaos. Courts inferred rules from their practices, but tensions damaged the business. LLC flexibility can empower founders, but lack of clarity can destroy friendships and companies alike.

LLC fiduciary duties mirror those in corporations but can be modified. Consider an investment LLC run by two siblings. They want to allow each other to pursue outside real estate deals without triggering conflicts of interest. Their operating agreement waives certain fiduciary duties, allowing competition so long as they disclose major transactions. In corporations, waiving fiduciary duties this broadly would be extremely difficult, if not impossible.

LLCs separate economic rights from management rights. A retired investor may own 40% of the LLC's profits but have no managerial authority. A non-member manager may run daily operations without owning equity. These flexible arrangements allow LLCs to reflect real human relationships.

At its heart, LLC governance is about tailoring control: shaping authority to match personalities, goals, and trust levels. It is law designed to follow the contours of human relationships instead of forcing them into rigid molds.

Conclusion

Management is where the personality of a business entity emerges. Corporations follow formal, well-defined structures, distributing power among shareholders, directors, and officers. Shareholders vote. Directors strategize. Officers act. Their roles are precise and deeply rooted in history.

LLCs follow a different philosophy. They allow members to design their governance like architects shaping a custom home. They choose how to divide authority, how to allocate profits, and how to balance relationships. Their flexibility empowers small businesses, families, partners, investors, and entrepreneurs to build frameworks that reflect their values and goals.

Both systems endure because both meet essential needs. Corporations excel in scale, predictability, and public investment. LLCs shine in versatility, speed, and intimacy. Understanding both illuminates not only business law, but human collaboration itself.

8 FIDUCIARY DUTIES WITHIN BUSINESS ASSOCIATIONS

Fiduciary duty is one of the most powerful ideas in business law and a frequent issue in business litigation. It is the law's way of saying that when people choose to work together in certain relationships—relationships built on trust, vulnerability, and shared enterprise—they must act with more care and loyalty than ordinary people in the marketplace. It is not enough to follow the bare minimum of contract law or to refrain from lying outright. Fiduciary duty demands the highest standards of honesty, diligence, selflessness, and fairness. It demands that individuals put the interests of the business, and of their partners, ahead of their own personal gain. It demands loyalty even when no one is watching, and care even when no one would know if corners had been cut. In short, it demands that people act not just as business participants, but as guardians of one another's hopes and investments.

This idea matters because business associations are built on relationships where people make themselves vulnerable. When three friends open a bakery together, they each trust the others to use shared funds wisely. When an investor elects directors to run a corporation, she trusts the directors to navigate risks responsibly. When members of an LLC choose a manager, they trust that manager to act in the company's best interests. Money becomes intertwined with trust, and trust becomes the foundation for thousands of decisions no contract could ever cover.

Among all business relationships, the partnership is where fiduciary duty appears in its purest form. General partners, unlike most corporate actors, have automatic fiduciary obligations simply by entering the relationship. Every partner is both a manager and an owner. Every partner has the power to bind the partnership. Every partner stands in a position of enormous trust. And because partnerships are so personal and so exposed—partners share liability, property, power, and risk—the law holds them to exceptionally high standards. Fiduciary duty is not an optional accessory in partnership law; it is the spine.

The Fiduciary Duties of General Partners

General partners owe two great fiduciary duties: the duty of loyalty and the duty of care. Courts sometimes separate these into smaller categories, often identifying the duty of good faith or the duty of disclosure, but almost all of these ideas flow naturally from loyalty and care. Loyalty prevents selfishness. Care prevents recklessness. Together, they are the guardrails that keep partnerships from becoming battlegrounds.

To understand these duties fully, imagine the partnership not as a legal abstraction, but as a story—a relationship between real people trying to build something together. Partnerships begin with excitement, ideas, and optimism. But they often end because of hidden conflicts, quiet resentments, or one partner's temptation to use the business for personal advantage. Fiduciary duty exists to prevent this story from turning tragic.

Consider three lifelong friends: Maya, Jonas, and Carlos. They grew up together, building homemade go-karts in the summers and selling lemonade on hot days. When they reach adulthood, they decide to form a general partnership to design sustainable playground equipment. They contribute equal capital and share responsibilities. Their partnership agreement is only six pages long. They trust each other so deeply that they barely read it.

The early months are filled with creativity. They sketch designs in coffee shops, pitch school districts, and negotiate with suppliers. But slowly, subtle dilemmas arise—dilemmas that will test each partner's loyalty, diligence, and honesty. These moments illustrate the fiduciary duties far better than any abstract definition.

The Duty of Loyalty

The duty of loyalty requires partners to put the partnership's interests ahead of their own personal gain, to avoid conflicts of interest, and to refrain from usurping opportunities that belong to the partnership. Courts often describe the duty of loyalty in near-moral terms. It is not enough for a partner to avoid stealing money out of the cash register. Loyalty demands that partners avoid situations where their personal interests compete with the partnership's interests, even if they believe they are acting fairly. Temptation itself is the danger.

Imagine Maya discovers that a school district wants to purchase $200,000 worth of playground equipment. She handles the negotiation and knows that the district is concerned about durability and maintenance costs. While researching suppliers, Maya privately realizes she could form a separate company—just a side venture—to manufacture durable maintenance kits. Without telling her partners, she starts the business quietly and offers the district a package deal: buy the playground equipment from the partnership and buy the maintenance kits from her new company.

In Maya's mind, this is harmless. The partnership benefits from the playground sale. Her side venture simply fills a need. But the law views this very differently. Maya has usurped a corporate opportunity. If maintenance kits relate to playground equipment—a central part of the partnership's business—then that opportunity belongs to the partnership, not to Maya individually. Her silence is fatal. By withholding the information, she violated her duty of loyalty.

Loyalty also prohibits partners from competing with the partnership. Suppose Jonas notices that a private school wants custom-designed climbing structures, something the partnership could build. Instead of pitching it through the partnership, he secretly accepts the job on weekends to earn extra cash. Even if he does a beautiful job, even if he believes the partnership is too busy to take the work, the law sees it clearly: Jonas competed with the partnership. He betrayed his partners' trust.

Then there is Carlos, who faces a different temptation. A supplier offers him a personal kickback of five percent if the partnership purchases materials exclusively through that supplier. Carlos thinks, No one will ever know. And besides, five percent won't hurt the partnership much. But even this small act violates the duty of loyalty. Carlos is using partnership resources to line his own pockets and creating a conflict of interest that could harm the partnership.

These examples show how loyalty is not simply about honesty. It is about structural commitment—choosing the partnership over personal gain every time a conflict arises. The duty of loyalty protects partnerships from being torn apart by quiet self-interest.

The Duty of Care

While the duty of loyalty prevents selfishness, the duty of care prevents recklessness. Partners must act with the care that an ordinarily prudent person would use in similar circumstances. In business terms, this means avoiding gross negligence, willful misconduct, or knowing violations of the law.

The duty of care is not about micromanaging every decision or punishing partners for ordinary mistakes. Every business involves risk. Every entrepreneur experiments, guesses, hopes, and occasionally fails. The duty of care is triggered when a partner fails to act with reasonable diligence or ignores obvious dangers.

Imagine that Jonas is responsible for managing the partnership's finances. He receives an email from a supplier offering an unbelievably good bulk discount on metal parts. Jonas is excited and impulsively wires $50,000 without checking whether the email is legitimate. It turns out to be a phishing scam. The money is gone.

Jonas did not act out of disloyalty—he received no personal benefit. But he violated the duty of care. A reasonably prudent person would have checked the supplier's identity or verified the invoice. His carelessness harmed the partnership.

In another episode, Maya chooses a more daring path. She reads a government report warning that a certain type of treated wood may soon be restricted due to safety concerns. She does not tell the other partners. She continues purchasing the wood because it is cheap and readily available. Months later, the regulation passes, the wood becomes illegal, and the partnership must spend thousands replacing hazardous materials in existing projects. Maya's failure to act on available information violated the duty of care.

Even Carlos, the most cautious of the three, struggles. He handles operational safety and notices that the sawdust ventilation system has been malfunctioning. The air feels heavier, but he tells himself it's fine. Instead of shutting down operations to inspect the system, he lets his employees keep working. A week later, a small fire breaks out from accumulated dust. No one is hurt, but the fire delays production and costs thousands in repairs. Carlos breached the duty of care by ignoring a known hazard.

These stories show how the duty of care operates not as a demand for perfection but as a demand for diligence. Partners must think before they act, investigate risks, communicate concerns, and behave like responsible stewards of the partnership's welfare.

The Duty of Good Faith and Fair Dealing

Some courts treat good faith as part of the duty of loyalty; others treat it as an independent requirement. Either way, good faith ensures honesty, transparency, and fairness in partnership dealings. Partners must not mislead one another, hide material facts, or manipulate processes for personal advantage.

Imagine a subtle betrayal. Jonas knows that the partnership is negotiating with a large private school network. He also knows that Carlos desperately wants to land the deal and has spent months preparing the proposal. Jonas, feeling jealous and wanting recognition, quietly delays sending Carlos's portion of the proposal to the superintendent. He tells himself, If the deal falls through, it'll encourage Carlos to work harder next time. But the superintendent interprets the delay as disrespect and awards the contract to a competitor.

Jonas did not steal money or divert a business opportunity. Yet his intentional obstruction violated the duty of good faith. He acted out of pettiness rather than partnership loyalty.

Even white lies can violate good faith. Maya once tells Jonas that a meeting with investors went "fine" even though the investors expressed major concerns about the business plan. She doesn't want to upset Jonas before his vacation. But her silence prevents the partnership from addressing the issues promptly, causing long-term harm. Good intentions do not excuse withholding material information.

The duty of good faith underscores the emotional and moral weight of partnership relationships. Partners must act not as adversaries, not as independent contractors, but as collaborators committed to shared goals.

The Duty of Disclosure

Fiduciary relationships thrive on honesty. Partners must disclose material information, especially when decisions depend on it. Disclosure is not merely about handing over financial statements; it is about being transparent when withholding information would harm the partnership.

Picture this situation: Maya learns through professional gossip that a major competitor is about to release a revolutionary playground design that could drastically reduce the partnership's market share. She dismisses the rumor, thinking it is unverified. Weeks later, the competitor launches the new product, catching the partnership off guard. Jonas and Carlos are blindsided. Maya's failure to disclose—even a rumor—violated her fiduciary duty because it deprived the partnership of a chance to prepare.

Disclosure obligations intensify when a partner stands to benefit personally. If Carlos learns that a supplier he privately invested in could be chosen for the next project, he must disclose his financial interest. Silence would taint the selection process with undisclosed conflict.

Disclosure is the antidote to mistrust. It is the lifeline that keeps partners connected as they navigate difficult decisions.

How Fiduciary Breaches Destroy Partnerships

Fiduciary breaches do not simply create legal liability;

they erode the emotional foundation of a partnership. Once partners begin to suspect one another of selfishness or carelessness, every decision becomes fraught. Meetings become tense. Emails become clipped. Ideas become guarded. A partnership once built on creativity becomes paralyzed by suspicion.

Imagine Maya, Jonas, and Carlos after months of tension. Maya resents Jonas for taking a side project. Jonas resents Carlos for his careless safety oversight. Carlos resents Maya for hiding information. Their once harmonious partnership becomes fragile. Eventually, they dissolve the partnership, selling off equipment and distributing remaining assets. They still care about each other personally, but the business is gone.

This story plays out in partnerships every day. Fiduciary duties exist not to punish wrongdoing but to prevent it—to preserve relationships, protect investments, and keep partners aligned.

Why Fiduciary Duties Matter So Deeply in Partnerships

Partnerships lack many of the structural protections found in corporations or LLCs. There are no directors to oversee operations, no officers to handle day-to-day decisions, no LLC operating agreement to customize duties. Partners stand alone with one another, bound not by hierarchy but by mutual trust.

This trust is powerful but fragile. Fiduciary duty is the law's way of reinforcing it, ensuring that partners treat each other not as competitors or strangers but as loyal allies in a shared enterprise.

In short, fiduciary duties are the quiet force that enables partnerships to survive the temptations, conflicts, and complexities of business life.

Fiduciary Duties of Corporate Officers and Directors

Fiduciary duty takes on a different shape when we move from partnerships into corporations. In partnerships, fiduciary obligations feel intimate, personal, and relational because partners operate shoulder to shoulder, sharing power equally. But in corporations, the world becomes larger and more structured. Power belongs not to individual owners, but to a board of directors and to officers who carry out the corporation's business. Shareholders may number in the thousands or millions, spread across cities and continents, connected only by a digital brokerage account. Such a vast and impersonal system requires a governance model capable of protecting investors who will never meet the people running their corporation. Fiduciary duty becomes that safeguard, a system of moral and legal guardrails that keeps the people in power from abusing the enormous trust placed in them.

Corporate fiduciary duties are built around the idea that directors and officers hold power on behalf of others. They do not own the corporation. They do not get to treat it as a personal bank account, a personal experiment, or a personal playground. Instead, they act as stewards of other people's money, responsible for directing vast resources, making strategic decisions, and managing risks with care, loyalty, and integrity. And because shareholders cannot monitor them directly, courts develop doctrines that protect against carelessness, conflicts of interest, manipulation, and self-dealing.

To understand these duties in living color, it helps to imagine the corporation not as a faceless entity but as a drama unfolding in conference rooms, email threads, late-night phone calls, and high-stakes decisions. It helps to see directors and officers not as abstract legal figures but as human beings with ambitions, fears, loyalties, blind spots, and flaws. The stories below bring fiduciary duty into this human landscape.

Consider Emberwave Technologies, a fast-growing corporation that manufactures wearable medical sensors. It began in a garage but now employs four hundred people, occupies three buildings, and reports to a board of directors composed of founders, investors, and outside experts. The corporation's officers handle daily operations, while the board sets strategic policy from a distance. At first glance, Emberwave seems like a shining success story. But beneath the surface, the corporation faces tensions that will test the fiduciary duties of its leaders.

The Duty of Care for Directors and Officers

The duty of care in corporate law requires directors and officers to be reasonably informed, to deliberate carefully, and to exercise the kind of judgment that a prudent person would use when managing their own affairs. It does not require omniscience or perfection, and it does not punish honest mistakes. Instead, it targets gross negligence, bad process, and reckless indifference.

To see how this works in practice, imagine the board of Emberwave Technologies preparing to vote on a major acquisition. Emberwave has grown quickly and wants to purchase a smaller company specializing in miniature sensor chips. The price is steep—$150 million—and the deal carries risks. The smaller company has patents that are still tied up in litigation. Some of its technology is untested. Still, the CEO is enthusiastic, and the board wants to keep pace with competitors.

During the board meeting, half the directors have not read the full due diligence report. One director skims it in the meeting itself. Another relies entirely on a short summary prepared by an assistant who does not understand the underlying technology. A third director simply trusts the CEO's excitement and nods along. After only twenty minutes of discussion, the board approves the acquisition unanimously.

Two years later, the patents are invalidated, the technology fails, and the corporation must write off the acquisition entirely. Shareholders file suit, arguing that the directors violated the duty of care. The issue is not the business outcome. The issue is the process. Directors must inform themselves, review available information, and ask questions. Their job is not to rubber-stamp management decisions but to deliberate with seriousness. Courts emphasize that directors must attend meetings, read reports, and understand risks before voting.

This principle also applies to officers. Imagine Emberwave's Chief Operating Officer, Dana, learns that one of the company's overseas factories has been ignoring safety protocols to speed up production. Dana does not investigate. She knows fixing the problem will slow shipments and anger the CEO. She tells herself the employees are overreacting. Months later, a worker is injured, triggering an expensive lawsuit and negative press. Dana's failure to investigate and correct a known risk is a breach of the duty of care.

The duty of care pushes directors and officers to take their roles seriously. It makes them responsible for the processes of decision-making, not just the outcomes. This principle is backed by the business judgment rule, which protects directors and officers when they make informed, good-faith decisions, even if those decisions turn out poorly. But the shield of the business judgment rule disappears when the process is reckless.

The Duty of Loyalty

If the duty of care focuses on competence, the duty of loyalty focuses on sincerity. Directors and officers must put the corporation's interests ahead of their own. They cannot use corporate opportunities for personal gain, cannot allow personal relationships to influence decisions, and cannot approve transactions in which they have a conflict of interest unless proper procedures are followed.

At Emberwave Technologies, loyalty becomes a battleground.

Consider the board's chair, Raymond, a charismatic industry veteran who helped shepherd Emberwave through its early days. As the company grows, Raymond's status gives him immense influence. Suppliers seek his approval. Investors listen eagerly when he speaks. But this influence creates temptation.

Suppose Raymond's cousin owns a consulting firm that claims it can streamline Emberwave's logistics. Raymond believes the cousin's company is competent, and he sees no harm in recommending them. He tells the board the consulting firm is "exceptional" without mentioning his family connection. The board approves a $5 million contract. Later, the consulting firm underperforms badly, causing delays and waste. When the connection comes to light, shareholders accuse Raymond of concealing a conflict of interest.

The violation is not in the recommendation. It is in the concealment. Directors must disclose conflicts so the board can evaluate transactions with clear eyes. If a conflict exists, the director must either recuse themselves or ensure the transaction meets statutory safeguards.

Now consider the CEO, Lila, a brilliant engineer whose

innovations built the company. Lila is approached privately by venture capitalists who want her to join a competing startup. They offer her stock options, a high salary, and a leadership role in developing a next-generation sensor. Lila considers the offer but keeps the negotiations secret. Meanwhile, she quietly delays Emberwave's own research in that direction. She tells herself that Emberwave is not ready, that the team is overworked, that delaying the project helps avoid burnout. In truth, she is clearing space for the opportunity she plans to take later.

Even before she accepts the new job, Lila has breached the duty of loyalty. She manipulated the corporation's affairs for personal advantage. She put her interests ahead of the corporation's. If she later joins the new startup and develops competing technology, her breach becomes even clearer. Corporate fiduciaries cannot exploit inside information, suppress projects, or manipulate strategy for their personal benefit.

Perhaps the most dramatic example of disloyalty in corporate history involves officers using secret side deals, shadow companies, or hidden compensation agreements. Imagine Emberwave's Chief Technology Officer, Erin, forming a separate company to buy specialized chips at a low price, then selling them to Emberwave with a 30% markup. Erin justifies this by saying the side company takes on the procurement risk. But her silence and secret profit violate the core of the duty of loyalty. Corporate opportunities do not belong to officers. They belong to the corporation.

The Corporate Opportunity Doctrine

A crucial part of the duty of loyalty is the corporate opportunity doctrine, which requires fiduciaries to offer business opportunities to the corporation before pursuing them personally. This doctrine creates dramatic fact patterns in real life, often involving brilliant but ambitious officers who convince themselves that their personal entrepreneurial visions align with the corporation's best interests.

Consider Emberwave's senior engineer, Noah, who develops a prototype for a small, wearable device that monitors hydration levels. The device fits naturally with Emberwave's product line, but Noah fears the corporation will be slow to develop it. He dreams of launching a startup where he can build the product himself. He shares the idea with his college friend rather than with Emberwave, and the two of them create a new company. The product becomes wildly successful. Emberwave later sues Noah, arguing that the opportunity belonged to the corporation.

Noah protests that Emberwave never asked for hydration-monitoring products. But fiduciary duty does not require the corporation to ask. It requires the fiduciary to offer. If the opportunity falls within the corporation's line of business, or if the corporation could reasonably pursue it, a fiduciary cannot seize it for themselves.

Good Faith and the Duty of Oversight

Good faith is sometimes treated as a separate duty, sometimes as part of loyalty, sometimes as part of care. Regardless of its classification, it protects corporations from leaders who act with dishonesty, intentional irresponsibility, or deliberate indifference.

One branch of good faith is the duty of oversight. Directors must monitor the corporation's compliance systems, internal controls, and risk-management processes. They do not need to micromanage employees, but they cannot ignore warning signs.

Imagine Emberwave starts receiving employee complaints about improper disposal of electronic waste. Some workers report that toxic materials are being dumped in regular trash bins to save time. The complaints reach the directors through quarterly compliance reports. A few directors glance at the reports but assume management is handling the issue. They never ask follow-up questions.

Months later, a whistleblower contacts regulators. Emberwave faces fines, bad publicity, and shareholder lawsuits. The directors may be liable for failing to exercise oversight. Courts describe this as a failure to implement or monitor reporting systems. Directors must ensure they receive information and that they act when red flags appear.

Good faith also forbids directors and officers from acting

with a purpose other than advancing the corporation's interests. If a director votes for a decision solely to harm a rival, or to curry favor with another board member, or to sabotage management, they violate good faith even if the transaction appears legitimate on paper.

How Fiduciary Breaches Unfold in Corporations

Corporate fiduciary breaches create ripples far beyond personal relationships. In a partnership, betrayal destroys the business and the trust among a handful of individuals. In a corporation, betrayal can harm thousands of shareholders, hundreds of employees, and entire communities.

When directors act carelessly, corporations stumble blindly into risky decisions. When officers act disloyally, they distort strategy for personal gain. When compliance systems are ignored, corporations commit unintentional violations that destroy reputations. These harms are structural, not personal. They undermine investor trust and destabilize the economy.

Consider Emberwave Technologies once more, now in crisis. The ill-fated acquisition resulted from a poor duty-of-care process. The CEO's secret job negotiations created internal instability. The CTO's side business inflated costs. The board ignored red flags about environmental compliance. Shareholders file lawsuits. Employees feel betrayed. The public wonders whether Emberwave can survive.

In this scenario, fiduciary duty becomes the thread connecting each failure. The corporation did not collapse because of one giant mistake. It collapsed because of many small breaches—echoes of selfishness, carelessness, and silence—that gradually hollowed out the structure. Fiduciary duties aim to prevent this slow erosion. They preserve the integrity of decision-making, the honesty of leadership, and the trust that makes investment possible.

Why Fiduciary Duty Matters in Corporations

Corporate fiduciary duties reflect the reality of modern business. Shareholders cannot sit in every boardroom or watch every officer's choices. They rely on fiduciary duties to ensure that directors and officers act with care, loyalty, honesty, and commitment. These duties act as the invisible scaffolding holding corporate governance together. They preserve fairness in a system built on delegation, separation of ownership and control, and massive financial interdependence.

At its core, fiduciary duty requires leaders to rise above the temptations that come with power. It asks them to act not as monarchs ruling a private kingdom, but as guardians entrusted with the well-being of others.

Fiduciary Duties of Limited Liability Company Members and Managers

Fiduciary duty in limited liability companies occupies a middle ground between the intimacy of partnerships and the formal hierarchy of corporations. LLCs are creatures of contract as much as creatures of statute, built on the idea that humans should be free to design their own business relationships. But this freedom does not eliminate trust. If anything, it creates a sharper need for honesty and loyalty, because the very governance structure often depends on personal agreements rather than rigid statutory commands. Unlike corporations, LLCs allow their members to modify fiduciary duties through operating agreements, sometimes limiting or even reshaping them entirely. But even with this flexibility, most LLCs still rely on default duties of loyalty, care, good faith, and disclosure to keep decision-makers honest and protect the business from self-serving behavior.

To understand the fiduciary duties of LLC members and managers, it helps to see the LLC not as a legal abstraction but as a living relationship—dynamic, human, and sometimes fragile. LLCs often form among friends, family members, business partners, or investors who believe they can achieve something greater together. These relationships begin with optimism but quickly become complicated as money flows, decisions accumulate, and personal interests collide. The stories below illuminate how fiduciary duties guide members and managers through these challenges, shaping the heart of LLC governance.

Imagine a small but ambitious LLC called Stonefield Spirits, founded by three friends—Ariana, Malik, and

Devon—who dream of producing artisanal whiskey using locally sourced grains. They rent a small warehouse, build a distillery system with their own hands, and pour their energy into crafting unique blends. The business grows steadily, gaining attention from restaurants and specialty liquor stores. They are proud and excited, but the expanding opportunities invite pressures they never anticipated. As the LLC evolves, so do the duties they owe each other and the business.

The Default Fiduciary Duties in Member-Managed LLCs

In member-managed LLCs, every member participates directly in the daily management of the business. This structure resembles a partnership, and the law often applies partnership-like fiduciary duties by default. Members owe one another loyalty, care, and good faith, even if the operating agreement is silent.

Consider Stonefield Spirits in its early days. With only three members, all decisions are made collectively. Ariana oversees production, Malik handles sales and marketing, and Devon manages finances. They trust each other deeply, so their operating agreement is only a few pages long. They do not bother to add provisions modifying fiduciary duties, assuming their friendship is enough to guide them.

But the business grows. A prominent restaurant chain wants Stonefield Spirits to create a private-label whiskey. This opportunity could double their revenue. Ariana, who develops the recipes, sees a chance to gain personal recognition. A celebrity chef involved with the restaurant chain encourages her to leave the LLC and join the chain directly, offering her a lucrative contract to develop products exclusively for them. Ariana is tempted. She thinks, The LLC will survive without me. And besides, I created the recipes—they're my work.

The temptation becomes a test of fiduciary duty. Because Stonefield Spirits is a member-managed LLC, Ariana owes the business a duty of loyalty. She cannot secretly pursue an opportunity that falls squarely within the LLC's line of business. She cannot use knowledge gained through the LLC to benefit herself at the company's expense. Even if she thinks the LLC is slow or disorganized, she must offer the opportunity to the LLC before acting on it personally. Her silence alone would be a breach.

This illustrates the central role that loyalty plays in LLCs. It prevents members from acting as competitors, using inside information for personal gain, or diverting opportunities that belong to the business. When members manage the business themselves, loyalty becomes the glue holding the group together.

The Duty of Loyalty in LLC Contexts

The duty of loyalty in LLCs may be modified or even waived in some jurisdictions, but unless the operating agreement changes it, the default duty resembles the partnership standard. It prevents members from engaging in self-dealing, competing with the LLC, or hiding conflicts of interest.

Stonefield Spirits offers a vivid set of examples. Malik, who handles sales, notices that a major distributor is interested in carrying whiskey from several small distilleries. The distributor quietly invites Malik to join as a consultant, promising him generous compensation if he helps recruit Stonefield Spirits and its competitors. Malik thinks the offer is harmless. The LLC will gain access to a major distributor, and he will earn side income.

But the conflict is deeper than that. Malik is using his role within the LLC to secure a personal opportunity. He cannot serve two masters. If he consults for the distributor, his financial loyalty shifts from Stonefield Spirits to the distributor's interests. He might be tempted to accept unfavorable terms to secure his consulting fee. Even more problematically, he gains insight into competitors the LLC may face in the future. This divided loyalty violates the fiduciary duty owed to the LLC.

Meanwhile, Devon faces a quieter but equally serious temptation. As the business expands, he handles the LLC's finances and begins paying himself additional "administrative fees" without telling the others. He tells himself that the distillery would collapse without his financial expertise. The fees are modest at first, but soon they grow. Devon thinks, I'll tell them eventually. I just need to make sure everything stays afloat.

But fiduciary duty does not allow secrecy. Devon must disclose his compensation, seek approval, and avoid hidden benefits. Even if he believes he deserves the money, the nondisclosure violates his duty of loyalty. Courts consistently hold that fiduciaries cannot take undisclosed compensation or unapproved benefits.

Loyalty in LLCs protects not only the business but the relationships on which the business relies. Without it, trust collapses quickly.

The Duty of Care in LLCs

The duty of care in LLCs resembles the corporate and partnership standard: members and managers must act with the diligence of a reasonably prudent person in similar circumstances. They must avoid gross negligence and willful misconduct. But in many states, operating agreements can modify the duty of care, often limiting liability for negligence.

In the absence of modification, the duty of care plays a crucial role, especially during growth phases.

A powerful example arises when Ariana experiments with a new distillation method. She wants to speed up production using a cheaper heating technique she learned online. The method is untested, and safety experts warn that improper use can cause pressure buildup. Ariana dismisses the warnings. She believes she knows better and begins using the method after hours, hoping to impress the others with her innovation.

One night, the still overheats. Pressure builds, a valve bursts, and the resulting explosion damages expensive equipment. No one is injured, but the LLC faces tens of thousands of dollars in repairs and lost production time. Ariana's conduct is not a simple mistake. It is reckless disregard for known risks, violating the duty of care.

In another instance, Devon notices that the LLC's insurance policy is about to lapse. He procrastinates renewing it, telling himself he will get to it later. Before he does, a delivery driver slips on spilled grain in the warehouse and is injured. Without insurance, the LLC faces a costly lawsuit. Devon's failure to act with reasonable diligence constitutes a breach of care.

The duty of care protects LLCs from the kind of silent failures—ignored warnings, overlooked deadlines, hasty judgments—that can cripple small businesses. It ensures that members and managers take reasonable steps to safeguard the enterprise.

Good Faith, Fair Dealing, and Honesty

Every LLC statute includes some version of a duty of good faith and fair dealing. Even if the operating agreement modifies or waives other duties, this one remains largely non-waivable. Good faith requires members and managers to act honestly, with a basic level of fairness, and without intentionally undermining the LLC.

Consider a moment of tension in Stonefield Spirits. Sales dip unexpectedly during a slow season. Malik, frustrated by Ariana's cautious expansion strategy, begins withholding information about new customer leads. He wants Ariana to look incompetent so he can argue for shifting more control of sales to himself. He does not lie outright; he simply omits key details. The result is predictable: Ariana makes decisions based on incomplete information, and the LLC misses crucial opportunities.

Even though Malik's conduct may not involve direct personal gain, his intentional obstruction violates the duty of good faith. Good faith prohibits vindictive or spiteful conduct that harms the enterprise.

Similarly, Ariana once tells Devon that a supplier demanded a price increase when, in reality, she negotiated the increase herself to build goodwill with the supplier for personal reasons. Her lie leads Devon to make budgeting decisions based on false information. Even if Ariana believed the lie was harmless, it breached the duty of good faith.

These examples show that good faith is not merely a moral obligation. It is a legal one. It prevents members from manipulating information, sabotaging decisions, or harming the business through intentional dishonesty.

Fiduciary Duties in Manager-Managed LLCs

In manager-managed LLCs, the dynamic shifts dramatically. The managers—not the members—bear primary fiduciary responsibilities. Members who are not managers generally have fewer duties, similar to passive shareholders in a corporation. This structure often arises when LLCs seek outside investment.

Imagine that Stonefield Spirits seeks to expand nationwide. The founders bring in several investors who contribute significant capital but do not want day-to-day involvement. The operating agreement names Ariana as the sole manager, with full authority over operations. Malik and Devon become members but no longer manage daily affairs. Several new investors also become passive members.

In this structure, Ariana owes fiduciary duties of loyalty and care to the LLC and its members. Malik and Devon, now passive members, owe limited duties unless they retain some management authority.

The shift creates new tensions. Imagine Ariana wants to open a second distillery in another state. She knows this expansion could dilute the original distillery's reputation. She also knows that her personal consulting business—Moonstone Beverage Advisors—would profit handsomely from managing the expansion project. She quietly proposes hiring Moonstone without disclosing that she owns it. The LLC signs a contract with Moonstone, paying significant consulting fees.

When the other members learn the truth, they are furious. Ariana's failure to disclose her interest in Moonstone violates the duty of loyalty. Manager-managed LLCs expect managers to be transparent about conflicts of interest.

On the duty of care side, imagine Ariana hires an inexperienced operations manager for the new facility because he is a close friend. She ignores warnings from Malik that the friend lacks relevant experience. As predicted, the new facility falls behind schedule, suppliers complain about poor communication, and quality declines. The LLC suffers significant financial loss. Ariana may have breached the duty of care by making a decision based on personal relationships rather than sound business judgment.

Manager-managed structures concentrate fiduciary obligations in a smaller group of people, increasing the stakes of each decision.

How Operating Agreements Shape Duties

One of the most distinctive aspects of LLC fiduciary law is the ability to modify or shape fiduciary duties through the operating agreement. Some agreements narrow the duty of loyalty, allowing members to pursue outside businesses or compete with the LLC so long as they disclose conflicts. Others limit liability for negligence, softening the duty of care. Still others specify how members must disclose information or how disputes will be resolved.

But these modifications require clarity. Courts often refuse to imply waivers of fiduciary duties. If an operating agreement wants to allow members to compete or engage in self-dealing, the language must be explicit. Ambiguity favors fiduciary obligations.

Imagine that Stonefield Spirits grows into a regional brand. The members want to allow each of them to operate private tasting rooms separate from the LLC's main business. If the operating agreement states vaguely that "members may pursue outside ventures," that may not be enough to waive the duty of loyalty. But if it states clearly that "members may open and operate private tasting rooms without offering such opportunities to the LLC," courts will honor the waiver.

This contractual freedom gives LLCs flexibility but also creates opportunities for misunderstanding. Poorly drafted agreements can leave members unsure of their obligations, increasing the likelihood of conflict.

How Fiduciary Breaches Affect LLCs

LLCs are often intimate organizations. They are built on relationships. Fiduciary breaches can therefore be emotionally devastating. When a friend, sibling, or trusted business partner acts selfishly or recklessly, the personal betrayal stings as deeply as the financial loss.

Imagine Stonefield Spirits after several years of growth. Ariana's secret negotiations, Malik's withheld information, and Devon's undisclosed compensation have all come to light. Trust collapses. Meetings become tense and unproductive. Emails turn curt. Decisions grind to a halt. Eventually, the members vote to dissolve the LLC. They liquidate assets, pay creditors, and divide what remains. A once-promising business ends not because of market forces but because fiduciary duties failed.

Why Fiduciary Duties Matter in LLCs

Fiduciary duties in LLCs provide the ethical and structural framework that helps the organization function. They protect members from exploitation, ensure transparency, safeguard investments, and anchor the trust necessary for collaboration. They keep opportunistic behavior in check, even when personal relationships strain under the pressure of business demands.

LLCs thrive because they offer freedom, flexibility, and creativity. But freedom without trust is chaos. Flexibility without loyalty is danger. Creativity without diligence is recklessness. Fiduciary duty is the quiet force that balances these competing energies, giving LLCs the stability they need to grow.

Conclusion: The Shared Soul of Fiduciary Duty Across Business Forms

Fiduciary duty is the hidden architecture that holds business organizations together. Whether we are watching general partners in a small creative venture, directors and officers guiding a billion-dollar corporation, or members and managers navigating the flexible world of LLCs, the same core principles appear again and again. Loyalty, care, honesty, good faith, and transparency form a universal language of trust. Each business form expresses these duties differently—

partnerships demand intimacy and shared commitment, corporations require structured oversight and independence, and LLCs offer customizable obligations shaped by human relationships and private agreements. But beneath these variations lies a common theme: whenever people entrust their money, hopes, and shared enterprise to someone else, the law steps in to protect that trust.

These duties are reflections of real human pressures. Partners feel the tug of personal opportunity. Directors are tempted by influence and shortcuts. LLC managers wrestle with the blurred boundaries between friendship and responsibility. Fiduciary duties stand as the law's quiet reminder that power must be used with integrity, that private interest must bow to shared purpose, and that business relationships cannot survive without honesty. They protect not only the financial health of an enterprise but the emotional bonds that allow people to collaborate in the first place.

Together, the three situations reveal a spectrum: from the intimate loyalty expected of partners, to the formal oversight required of corporate leaders, to the flexible but still demanding duties of LLC members and managers. Every business form embodies a different vision of trust and risk, but all rely on fiduciary duty to keep ambition aligned with fairness. In the end, fiduciary duty is the moral center of business associations—the compass that guides people not just to work together, but to work together well.

9 SHAREHOLDER AND MEMBER LITIGATION

Shareholder and member litigation rarely emerges from dry legal disputes. It grows out of human frustration, strained relationships, and moments of genuine uncertainty about who holds power and who has been wronged. Corporations and LLCs are built on trust. When that trust cracks, owners begin to ask the law for answers. The central question in these lawsuits is deceptively simple: who is suing whom, and for what injury? The law divides these disputes into direct and derivative claims, and although the distinction may seem abstract at first, it determines nearly every aspect of a lawsuit. Understanding these categories requires exploring not only the legal rules but the human stories behind them, because real-world conflicts illuminate why the doctrine matters and how courts apply it.

Direct Litigation

Direct litigation arises when a shareholder or LLC member suffers a personal injury that does not fall equally on all other owners. It is rooted in the idea that certain rights—such as the right to vote shares, receive promised distributions, inspect books, or rely on truthful statements when purchasing interests—belong to individuals rather than to the business as a whole. When those personal rights are violated, the injured person may bring a direct suit.

To see this more clearly, imagine Goldenfield Robotics, a fast-growing corporation founded by four engineers who once worked side-by-side in a garage. As the company grew into a sophisticated operation with investors and a formal board, relationships among the founders shifted. Alex became CEO, and his approach to leadership sometimes clashed with the more collaborative mindset the group once shared. One day, during a critical vote on whether the corporation should acquire a smaller competitor, Alex instructs the corporate secretary not to count Jules's shares. He claims a vague "transfer restriction" disqualifies Jules from voting. No such restriction exists. Jules suffers a personal injury: he alone is denied the right to vote his shares. His harm is not shared with other shareholders, and his lawsuit would be a direct action seeking restoration of his personal voting rights.

Direct suits often involve misrepresentations made to

individual shareholders. Suppose Goldenfield raises new capital by selling shares to outside investors. During the offering, officers claim the company's patents are fully secure and a lucrative government contract is on the verge of approval. Both statements are false. Investors who relied on these statements suffer a personal economic injury tied to their decision to purchase shares. Their claims arise from individualized harm, not from collective harm to the corporation, and therefore are direct.

The same principles apply to LLCs, although the analysis often depends on the operating agreement. Consider Sweet Hearth Company, a prosperous bakery owned by two sisters, Dara and Leila. When family tension spills into business operations, Leila stops issuing distributions to Dara. The bakery itself is thriving, and the operating agreement entitles each sister to a proportional share of profits. Dara's right to distributions is personal. The injury affects her alone. Her claim is direct because it concerns her individual entitlement rather than the LLC's financial condition.

Direct claims can also arise from denied access to company information. If Dara requests financial records, and Leila refuses her access in violation of statutory rights or the operating agreement, Dara suffers a personal injury. Her interest as a member includes the right to inspect certain documents. A lawsuit enforcing that right is direct.

These examples show that direct litigation protects the personal rights owners hold against the business and against each other. When those rights are violated, the harm belongs to the individual. The lawsuit belongs to the individual. And any remedy flows directly to the plaintiff, not the business.

Derivative Litigation

Derivative litigation, by contrast, arises when the primary injury is to the corporation or the LLC. Shareholders or members may feel the financial consequences of that injury, but their harm is indirect, flowing from the diminished value of the business rather than any personal right. Because the business is the direct victim, the lawsuit must be brought on behalf of the business. If the suit succeeds, any recovery goes back into the corporate or LLC treasury.

Return to Goldenfield Robotics. Suppose Mateo, the CFO, creates a shell company and funnels corporate funds into it under the guise of "consulting fees." The corporation loses substantial assets. This is not a personal injury to Priya or any other shareholder. It is an injury to Goldenfield. When Priya sues, she must bring a derivative action, standing in the corporation's shoes and seeking restoration of corporate assets.

Derivative litigation also arises when insiders engage in self-dealing or waste corporate resources. Imagine the CEO signs a contract with a supplier owned by his brother. The supplier charges wildly inflated prices, draining corporate funds. All shareholders suffer indirectly because the corporation's value is harmed. Such claims—alleging breach of fiduciary duty, waste, or unfair dealing—are derivative because the corporation itself is the injured party.

Because derivative suits involve the business's rights rather than the owner's rights, they come with additional procedural hurdles. The most important is the demand requirement. Before filing suit, a shareholder must usually demand that the board take action. The idea is simple: the corporation's affairs are normally controlled by its board, not by individual shareholders. Only when the board refuses or is too conflicted to act may a shareholder bring a derivative action. In some cases, demand is excused because it would be futile. If the board members themselves participated in the wrongdoing or are closely tied to the person who did, asking them to sue would make no sense. In Goldenfield, if the board is composed of Mateo's supporters or relatives, Priya may bypass the demand requirement.

LLC derivative litigation follows similar principles but is often shaped by the operating agreement. Suppose Sweet Hearth Company experiences misappropriation: Leila secretly uses $80,000 of LLC funds to renovate a personal property, disguising the spending as "kitchen improvements." The LLC loses money. Vendors complain of delayed payments. Creditors increase their interest rates. The harm belongs to the LLC. Dara's claim must be brought derivatively, seeking to restore the stolen funds to the company.

Even negligence by management typically creates a derivative claim. Imagine Leila ignores clear safety warnings in the bakery and an employee suffers a serious injury during a rush-hour shift. The LLC faces legal liability and financial strain. Dara experiences the consequences only because the LLC is harmed. Her claim is therefore derivative.

The emotional roots of derivative suits mirror those of direct suits but are often more intense because they arise when owners feel powerless to stop harm to the business. Priya sues because she believes the business is being looted. Dara sues because she fears Sweet Hearth is being mismanaged into the ground. Derivative suits reflect a breakdown in governance: those who normally protect the entity fail to act, so owners step in to protect the business they have invested in.

Some cases blur the line between direct and derivative harm. For example, if Goldenfield issues new stock only to insiders at a steep discount, outside shareholders experience dilution. Although this feels like a personal injury, courts usually treat dilution as harm to the corporation because the issuance itself violated corporate norms. Only rarely do courts permit a dual or hybrid claim. Most of the time, they require plaintiffs to choose one category.

Ultimately, the distinction between direct and derivative litigation shapes who controls the lawsuit, what procedures apply, who receives any recovery, and how courts review the claims. Direct suits protect personal rights. Derivative suits protect the business itself. Together, they form a balanced system of accountability within business associations. Direct claims shine a spotlight on moments when individuals are singled out or personally harmed—like Jules losing his vote or Dara losing her distributions. Derivative claims illuminate injuries to the entity, like Mateo's misappropriation or Leila's misuse of LLC funds, which threaten the business's survival and thereby affect everyone.

Shareholder and member litigation reveals the fault lines inside corporations and LLCs. It highlights where trust falters and where power is abused. The doctrines of direct and derivative suits help courts separate personal grievances from structural injuries, ensuring that the right party receives the right remedy. For students of business law, mastering this distinction offers insight into how the law protects both individual rights and the integrity of the business itself. It also provides a window into the psychology of failing business relationships, where lawsuits become not merely legal tools but expressions of frustration, betrayal, and the struggle for control. Understanding who is suing whom, and why, is essential for navigating the complex and deeply human world of business disputes.

10 LIABILITY RULES

Liability rules in business associations tell the story of who bears the cost when things go wrong. Every business form—partnership, corporation, or LLC—offers its own blend of protection and responsibility, and those boundaries matter most when a dispute erupts or a debt comes due. These rules act like the contour lines of a map: they show where personal risk begins, where it ends, and when the law will reach past an entity to hold individuals accountable. Understanding liability is not just about memorizing statutes; it's about understanding how power, decision-making, trust, and fairness interact within each business form. In the pages that follow, we will explore how general partners face sweeping personal liability, how corporate officers and directors may be exposed for misconduct or neglect, how LLC members and managers navigate a carefully balanced shield, and how courts sometimes pierce that shield entirely.

Together, these doctrines reveal the deeper logic of business law: its constant effort to encourage enterprise while preventing individuals from hiding behind the structures they create.

Liability of General Partners Under the Revised Uniform Partnership Act (1997)

General partnerships remain one of the most human forms of business association. They are built on trust, shared ambition, casual conversations that grow into plans, and a willingness to combine talent and resources. Yet RUPA imposes some of the most sweeping personal liability rules in modern business law. Understanding these rules requires not only reading statutory language but watching how real people experience partnership life, how simple decisions create complex exposure, and how one person's mistake can alter the financial fate of everyone involved.

Personal Liability for Partnership Obligations

Under RUPA, the partnership is a legal entity distinct from its partners. It owns property, enters contracts, and can sue or be sued. But even with this entity status, general partners remain personally liable for the obligations of the partnership. This liability is joint and several, which means that a creditor may choose to pursue any one partner for the entire debt. It is an unforgiving rule, and many new business owners underestimate its reach.

Consider the story of Sam and Ethan, who start Green Horizon Yardworks, a friendly neighborhood landscaping business. Their partnership is informal, built on a handshake and trust. They split profits, share tools, and begin advertising. When they take out a loan to buy a second truck, the lender relies not just on the promise of future landscaping revenue but on Sam's and Ethan's personal assets. Their savings accounts and even their homes sit quietly as collateral behind the scenes. It feels harmless until the day Ethan forgets to secure a lawn mower in the back of the truck, and it crashes into a parked car. The partnership is liable for the accident, and when Green Horizon cannot fully pay the judgment, the car owner turns to both Sam and Ethan personally. Sam was nowhere near the accident, yet he faces the same financial risk because partnership liability binds him just as tightly as Ethan.

Another example illustrates how routine business decisions can swell into personal burdens. Lila and Brennan open a vintage clothing shop called ThreadQuest. They sign a three-year lease on a storefront in a trendy district because they believe foot traffic will be strong. But the neighborhood's energy fades, sales decline, and they fall behind on rent. When the landlord sues, the partnership is liable first. But when the partnership's assets prove insufficient, the landlord seeks full payment from Brennan, even though Lila had been the one to push aggressively for the lease. Under RUPA, it does not matter whose idea the lease was. A partner's signature binds all partners, and their personal liability stands equal.

These examples reveal why general partnerships require extraordinary trust. The law expects partners to take responsibility for each other's decisions, which can either create deep solidarity or deep stress. The rule protects creditors and encourages commerce, but it places enormous weight on the shoulders of partners who may never have imagined the consequences when they shook hands over a business idea.

Liability for Wrongful Acts and Breaches of Trust

RUPA also makes partners personally liable for wrongful acts committed by any partner in the ordinary course of business. This includes negligence, intentional torts, and breaches of trust. In practice, partners often discover that they are responsible for behavior they would never have chosen themselves.

Take the story of City Harvest Events, a thriving catering partnership run by three partners: Jordan manages hiring, Mae oversees food preparation, and Ravi handles client relations. One season, exhausted by the pace of wedding events, Jordan becomes careless and stops conducting proper background checks. He hires an employee with a history of violent behavior. During a corporate banquet, the new hire assaults a guest. The guest sues the partnership. Even though Mae and Ravi had no role in hiring, and even though Jordan feels tremendous remorse, all three partners face personal liability once partnership assets are exhausted. The public should not bear the risk of internal mistakes, so the law shifts that risk onto the partners.

This rule also applies when a partner commits a breach of trust. Imagine Stonebridge Property Group, a real estate partnership that manages rental properties. One partner, Lena, is responsible for tenant deposits. Under financial stress, she begins "borrowing" from the deposit fund, thinking she will repay it soon. But the debts grow, and tenants begin moving out. When their deposits cannot be returned, lawsuits follow. The innocent partners find themselves personally liable for Lena's wrongdoing. They did not know about the missing funds, and they never benefited from the breaches, but RUPA attaches liability to all partners because the partnership held itself out as a unified business. The emotional fallout is immediate. Accusations fly. Friendships strain. Even marriages feel the impact. Many partnerships do not survive the betrayal.

The principle also applies to negligent acts committed in the ordinary course of business. If Sam from Green Horizon accidentally injures a passerby while carrying equipment, Ethan is personally liable despite having no involvement in the accident. Similarly, if Heidi and Caleb run Aurora Floral together and Caleb impulsively agrees to supply flowers at a steep discount for a major hotel, Heidi is on the hook even if she begged Caleb for months to stop making unilateral promises. The rule is simple: each partner is an agent of the partnership, and the partnership is bound by their actions. But living with that rule is emotionally complex, especially when one partner feels consistently blindsided by the decisions of another.

Liability for Incoming and Withdrawing Partners

RUPA attempts to bring fairness to partnership liability by distinguishing the obligations of incoming and departing partners. New partners are not personally liable for obligations incurred before they joined. This creates some protection, but the protection is narrow. The moment a new partner joins, they are personally liable for any new debt the partnership incurs.

Imagine an advertising partnership called BrightLine Creative, run by two founders who have struggled to attract stable clients. They recruit Naomi, a talented designer, to join as a partner, assuring her that the worst financial problems are behind them. Naomi gladly accepts and throws herself into the work. But as soon as she becomes a partner, she becomes personally liable for new obligations. When the firm leases new equipment and hires contractors for a risky campaign, Naomi becomes personally responsible for those debts. If BrightLine collapses a year later, creditors may pursue her personal assets. Naomi did nothing wrong, yet she bears the burden of the partnership's decisions simply because she agreed to join. Many new partners are shocked to discover how quickly their liability expands once they sign a partnership agreement.

Departing partners face their own challenges. Under

RUPA, a partner is not personally liable for obligations incurred after their withdrawal, but only if third parties have notice of that withdrawal. Without proper notice, the withdrawing partner can remain personally liable for debts or contracts formed long after leaving the business. Suppose Brennan leaves ThreadQuest after tensions rise with Lila. He assumes his departure frees him from future liability. But if they never notify suppliers or lenders, those parties may continue relying on Brennan's involvement. When Lila later orders inventory on credit and cannot pay, creditors may pursue Brennan personally, even though he played no role in the order and had no knowledge of it. This rule protects third parties who acted in good faith, but it often surprises withdrawing partners who believed their relationship with the business had ended for good.

These liability rules influence every aspect of partnership culture. They shape how partners communicate, how they divide responsibilities, and how they decide whether to trust one another. They create urgency around written agreements and transparency. They push partners to consider formal structures—like LLCs—when the risks feel too great. Yet partnerships continue to thrive because for many people, the simplicity and human closeness of the partnership form outweigh the dangers. They believe that shared responsibility strengthens them and that partnership liability is manageable when trust is strong.

In the end, the liability of general partners under RUPA

tells a story of shared fate. Partnerships ask individuals to combine their talents and assets, and in return, the law binds them to one another's decisions. When partners communicate well and respect each other, this shared liability creates unity. When they falter, the repercussions reach into every corner of their personal and financial lives. Understanding these doctrines helps students see partnerships as they truly are: not just business entities, but human relationships built on faith, risk, and the profound weight of mutual responsibility.

Liability of Corporate Officers and Directors Under the Model Business Corporation Act (2016)

Corporations may seem like sleek, impersonal machines compared to partnerships, but they are ultimately guided by human beings who make choices, set priorities, and take risks that can profoundly affect others. The Model Business Corporation Act of 2016 provides the framework for understanding when those individuals—corporate officers and directors—may be personally liable for harm to the corporation, its shareholders, or third parties. The rules are designed to encourage responsible management while also protecting corporate leaders from lawsuits that could chill thoughtful decision-making. Yet even with these protections, liability arises in ways that are often surprising, human, and deeply tied to the pressures of running a business. Understanding the liability of officers and directors requires entering their world: boardrooms full of tension, hurried decisions, ethical crossroads, and moments when judgment falters or loyalty drifts.

The Boundary Between Corporate Risk and Personal Liability

Directors and officers are often shielded from personal liability by one of the most powerful doctrines in corporate law: the business judgment rule. This rule gives them protection when they make honest, informed, and good-faith decisions—even if those decisions turn out disastrously. The law recognizes that business is risky. Corporations need leaders willing to take calculated risks without the constant fear of personal lawsuits. Yet the boundary between protected judgment and personal liability becomes clear only when a decision crosses into bad faith, neglect, or intentional wrongdoing.

Consider the story of Northern Pine Outfitters, a rapidly growing outdoor-gear company headquartered near a national park. The board of directors consists of five members, each with different strengths and personalities. Angela, the chair, is visionary but sometimes impatient. Mark, the CFO, is cautious and analytical. Two independent directors provide measured guidance, while the CEO, Rita, balances operational realities with strategic ambitions. Together, they face a major decision when a foreign distributor offers to place Northern Pine's products in hundreds of stores overseas. The proposal promises enormous growth but requires a substantial investment and carries political risk because of the distributor's ties to a volatile government.

The board debates for hours. Angela is enthusiastic. Mark expresses serious concerns. The independent directors request more information. After reviewing financial projections, market data, and legal opinions, the board votes to move forward. Months later, political unrest erupts in the distributor's region. Shipments stall. The distributor collapses. Northern Pine loses millions. Shareholders are furious and sue the directors, claiming negligence.

But under the business judgment rule, the directors are protected. They acted in good faith, considered relevant information, sought expert advice, and made a rational decision. The business judgment rule does not require them to be right; it requires them to act responsibly. The case is dismissed.

Yet the protections of the business judgment rule do not cover every scenario. Imagine the same board facing a different decision. Suppose that, instead of conducting a careful analysis, Angela pushes for a rushed vote on a similarly risky expansion deal, arguing that she "has a good feeling" and cannot wait for further review. Mark begs for time to gather more information, but Angela insists. The board, intimidated by her confidence and weary from the long day, approves the deal without reviewing critical financial documents. Months later, the project collapses, costing the company millions. This time, shareholders have a strong claim that the directors breached their duty of care by failing to act on an informed basis. The business judgment rule cannot shield decisions made in haste, without adequate investigation.

Personal liability may still be avoided if the directors can show that the corporation's exculpation clause protects them from monetary damages for breaches of the duty of care. Many corporations adopt such clauses. But exculpation never protects against bad faith, intentional misconduct, or knowing violations of law. When decision-making crosses into these darker territories, the liability shield falls away.

Liability Arising From Breaches of Loyalty and Good Faith

The most serious liability for corporate officers and directors arises when they breach their duty of loyalty or act in bad faith. The duty of loyalty requires leaders to put the corporation's interests ahead of their own and to avoid conflicts of interest. The duty of good faith demands honesty, transparency, and adherence to the corporation's welfare. When these duties are broken, personal liability becomes not only possible but likely.

One memorable example involves a fictional technology corporation called Blue Ember Systems. Its board includes a charismatic director named Colin, who operates a private consulting firm on the side. When Blue Ember begins searching for a software vendor to modernize their internal systems, Colin quietly steers the board toward a small firm in which he owns a hidden stake. He aggressively promotes the firm's capabilities, dismissing concerns from other directors, and votes in favor of awarding them the contract. He does not disclose his financial interest. When the vendor performs poorly, crashes the company's network twice, and ultimately causes severe operational losses, shareholders launch a lawsuit.

Colin's failure to disclose his conflict of interest constitutes a classic breach of loyalty. The business judgment rule cannot protect him because he acted for personal gain and concealed material information. He is personally liable for damages. The other directors may escape liability if they reasonably relied on Colin's misleading statements, but they will undergo scrutiny to determine whether they should have recognized warning signs.

Bad faith also exposes directors to liability. Imagine a pharmaceutical corporation, Riverview Biotech, facing mounting pressure to produce a new drug quickly. The director responsible for safety oversight, Dr. Lena, discovers early reports indicating serious potential side effects. Afraid of delaying production and losing investor support, she suppresses the warnings and instructs her team to "focus on positive data." When the drug reaches the market and patients suffer injuries, lawsuits rain down on the corporation. Dr. Lena faces personal liability because she knowingly ignored significant risks and violated her duty to act in good faith. Her choices went beyond carelessness; they reflected intentional disregard for the corporation's legal and ethical obligations.

Officers, unlike directors, also face liability when they personally participate in wrongful conduct. Suppose the CEO of a regional grocery chain knowingly approves fraudulent accounting entries to inflate quarterly results. When regulators discover the scheme, the corporation pays heavy fines, and shareholders suffer losses. Because the CEO actively participated in the fraud, she is personally liable. Unlike directors, officers cannot claim the protection of pure oversight; their direct involvement exposes them more immediately.

Liability to Third Parties and the Reach of Personal Responsibility

Liability of directors and officers does not arise solely from internal governance failures. They can also face personal liability to third parties, though the circumstances are narrow. A central principle of corporate law is that directors and officers are not personally liable for corporate debts or corporate breaches of contract simply because they hold leadership positions. Yet they may be liable for torts they personally commit or participate in, or for wrongful acts they authorize or ratify.

Consider a small construction corporation called Redwood BuildCo, run by a respected director named Hannah and an operations officer named Marco. Redwood agrees to build a series of custom homes for a developer. Unbeknownst to Hannah, Marco begins cutting corners to save money—using cheaper materials, skipping inspections, and ignoring safety rules. One of the houses collapses during construction, injuring a subcontractor. Lawsuits follow. The corporation is liable, but Marco is personally liable as well because he personally directed the negligent acts. Hannah may avoid liability if she had no reason to suspect wrongdoing and reasonably relied on Marco's reports. But if she ignored red flags—such as repeated complaints or missing inspection records—she could face liability for negligent supervision.

Directors and officers may also become personally responsible for corporate actions if they knowingly violate statutory duties. Suppose Evergreen BankCorp must make certain regulatory filings. The chief compliance officer, Brian, is fully aware of the deadlines but intentionally delays submitting the documents to avoid revealing losses. Regulators impose penalties and shareholders experience stock price declines. Brian may be personally liable because he knowingly violated legal requirements.

A particularly dramatic example involves environmental violations. Imagine ClearRiver Bottling Co., a corporation that operates a water-bottling facility near a protected wetland. The operations officer, Tessa, realizes that a malfunctioning filtration system is releasing contaminants into nearby streams. Afraid of causing public alarm or triggering expensive repairs, she instructs staff to "keep the system running" and delay filing incident reports. When the contamination becomes public, ClearRiver faces massive fines. Tessa is personally liable for knowingly participating in environmental violations. The directors may also face liability if they failed to implement reasonable systems to detect or prevent such misconduct.

These stories show that personal liability for directors and officers is not an everyday occurrence. Most corporate decisions, even flawed ones, remain protected by the business judgment rule. Liability emerges only when leaders cross important boundaries: ignoring critical information, concealing conflicts, acting for personal gain, participating in wrongdoing, or placing the corporation in knowing violation of the law. These boundaries preserve both accountability and the freedom to make bold decisions.

In the end, the liability rules of the MBCA reflect a careful balance. Corporations need leaders willing to innovate, expand, and make difficult choices without fear of personal ruin. But they also need safeguards against selfishness, dishonesty, and recklessness. Directors and officers hold immense power. Their decisions shape not only the fate of the corporation but the lives of employees, shareholders, customers, and communities. Liability doctrines remind them that this power carries responsibility. The law protects those who act with honesty, diligence, and loyalty. It disciplines those who betray the trust placed in them.

Liability of Limited Liability Company Members and Managers Under the Uniform Limited Liability Company Act (2013)

Limited liability companies have become the favored business form for new ventures, small businesses, family enterprises, and sophisticated investment structures alike. Their promise is simple and powerful: the flexibility of a partnership combined with the liability protection of a corporation. Yet the Uniform Limited Liability Company Act of 2013, often known as the ULLCA, makes clear that this protection is not absolute. Members and managers are shielded from the LLC's debts, but the shield has seams and conditions. When those seams tear—by statute, conduct, or agreement—personal liability can emerge. Understanding when and why this happens requires looking closely at the rules and, even more importantly, at the human decisions that cause those rules to matter.

The Promise and Limits of Limited Liability

The most appealing feature of an LLC is right there in the name: limited liability. Under the ULLCA, members are not personally liable for the LLC's obligations solely because they are members. Managers are not personally liable simply by serving as managers. The concept sounds clean and comforting. But in real-world business life, it is rarely that simple. Liability protections rise or fall on how people act, what they agree to, and the circumstances of each decision.

Imagine an LLC called Blue Harbor Kayaks, founded by

two friends, Priya and Leo. They rent waterfront space, build customized kayaks, and offer guided tours. They choose the LLC form because they want protection from personal liability if someone is injured during a tour. The operating agreement states that Blue Harbor Kayaks is manager-managed, with Leo serving as the sole manager. Priya is a passive member, assisting occasionally but not formally running the business.

One summer afternoon, a sudden storm blows in during a guided tour. A kayak capsizes, injuring a customer. The LLC is sued for negligence. Under ULLCA, the LLC is liable. But Priya and Leo are not personally responsible for the LLC's debts simply because they are members or managers. Their homes, savings, and personal property remain separate. This is precisely the protection they sought.

But this protection is not limitless. Suppose Leo hired the tour guide without conducting background checks, even though the operating agreement required vetting all employees. Or suppose Priya, despite being a passive member, personally promises a customer that the LLC will refund all fees if anything goes wrong. The analysis begins to shift. The shield of limited liability remains strong when members and managers act within the bounds of their roles and the law. But when they step outside those bounds, liability creeps closer.

The ULLCA provides the framework, but life provides the scenarios that test it.

Personal Liability for One's Own Conduct

The ULLCA draws a clear line: members and managers are not personally liable for the LLC's obligations, but they are responsible for their own wrongful acts. If a member personally commits a tort, participates in wrongdoing, or directs others to do so, limited liability does not protect them. The LLC shields them from vicarious liability for the acts of others, but not from liability for their own behavior.

Consider a brewery and taproom called Red Willow Ales, owned by three members: Jake, who serves as head brewer; Carla, who handles marketing; and Darius, who serves as manager under a manager-managed operating agreement. The business attracts a devoted local following, but rapid growth brings growing pains. One afternoon, Jake decides to rush a batch of beer to meet demand. He bypasses a key sanitation step, thinking it "probably won't matter." The batch becomes contaminated, sickening several customers. The LLC faces claims, but Jake may face personal liability as well because he personally engaged in negligent conduct. The ULLCA protects Jake from liability for obligations arising solely from his membership status, but it does not shield him from liability for his own negligence.

A different scenario reveals the role of managerial responsibility. Suppose Darius, as manager, knowingly approves false advertising claims stating that Red Willow's beers contain "zero allergens," even though he is aware that cross-contamination occasionally occurs in the brewery. A customer with a severe allergy suffers a reaction and sues. Darius cannot hide behind the LLC structure. He is personally liable because he personally engaged in a wrongful act.

Members and managers may also be liable for fraud, misrepresentation, or intentional misconduct. Imagine a real estate development LLC called Silver Ridge Estates. Two managing members, Tanya and Victor, promote a new housing project to investors. They knowingly inflate projected rental income, claiming that local businesses have committed to leasing nearby retail space when no such agreements exist. Investors rely on the false statements and lose their money. Under ULLCA, both Tanya and Victor face personal liability because they personally committed fraudulent acts.

But not all personal liability stems from dramatic misconduct. Sometimes it arises from small decisions made carelessly. Suppose a managing member of a cleaning-services LLC carelessly leaves a bucket of water on a customer's floor, causing a slip-and-fall injury. The LLC is liable, but the individual member is also personally liable. The line between protected and unprotected behavior lies in the difference between being a passive owner and personally causing harm.

The lesson is simple but profound: the LLC protects members and managers from liability for business debts and obligations, but it does not absolve them of responsibility for their own acts. The ULLCA reflects a balance between encouraging business formation and ensuring accountability for individual behavior.

Personal Liability Through Assumption, Guarantees, and Improper Conduct

Even with the strong protections of limited liability, members and managers can become personally liable through three pathways: voluntarily assuming liability, voluntarily guaranteeing obligations, or engaging in conduct that justifies piercing the liability shield entirely. These pathways require careful attention because they often appear in moments of trust, haste, or optimism.

One common pathway arises through personal guarantees. Suppose two childhood friends, Maya and Theo, start an LLC called Hearthstone Coffee Roasters. They lease a roasting facility and seek a loan to purchase equipment. The bank likes their concept but wants additional security. It insists that Maya personally guarantee the loan. Maya signs the guarantee because she believes in the business and trusts Theo. Years later, when the LLC faces financial strain and cannot repay the loan, the bank invokes Maya's guarantee. She becomes personally liable for the full debt, even if Theo contributed to the financial difficulties and even if the LLC still exists. The LLC structure provides no protection because Maya voluntarily agreed to personal liability.

Assumption of liability occurs when members act outside

their authority in ways that bind themselves rather than the LLC. Imagine that Theo, without consulting Maya or following the operating agreement, signs a contract promising that the LLC "and its members personally" will pay a distributor for coffee beans. The distributor relies on that language. When the LLC later disputes the bill, the distributor pursues Theo personally. He assumed liability through his own conduct, and the LLC structure cannot shield him.

The most dramatic pathway to personal liability is the judicial doctrine of piercing the LLC veil, which will be explored more deeply in a later chapter. Still, the doctrine is worth touching on here because it represents the most extreme consequence of improper conduct. Piercing occurs when members abuse the LLC form so completely that it becomes an instrument of fraud or injustice. Courts may disregard the separateness of the LLC and hold members personally liable, much like piercing the corporate veil.

Examples help illustrate when this happens. Consider a small trucking LLC called SilverStar Transport. The sole member, Harper, treats the business like her personal wallet, paying her household bills from the business account, failing to keep records, and ignoring filing requirements. She leaves the LLC undercapitalized and uses it as a shield to avoid obligations to creditors. When a truck accident results in large claims, the injured parties argue that the LLC is simply Harper's alter ego. Because she ignored corporate formalities, blurred financial lines, and used the LLC for improper purposes, a court may pierce the veil and hold her personally liable.

Another scenario involves a property-management LLC called Meadowbrook Rentals. Its two members, Alan and Nina, deliberately move funds out of the LLC bank account to evade creditor claims, leaving the LLC insolvent. A court may hold both members personally responsible if it finds that they looted the LLC and acted to undermine its separate existence. These outcomes are rare but serve as warnings: LLCs provide limited liability only when members respect the boundaries between personal affairs and business affairs.

Even without veil-piercing, the ULLCA allows members and managers to be liable for wrongful distributions. Suppose Meadowbrook Rentals distributes profits to Alan and Nina even though the LLC cannot meet its debts. Under ULLCA, members who receive such improper distributions may be required to return them. This liability is not punitive; it is corrective, ensuring that creditors are not unfairly harmed by premature or excessive payouts.

These pathways to liability—guarantees, assumptions, and misconduct—illustrate that limited liability is conditional, not absolute. Many LLC founders believe that the structure protects them from all personal exposure, only to discover that everyday decisions can pull them outside the shield. The ULLCA encourages entrepreneurship by protecting members from vicarious liability, but it simultaneously demands respect for boundaries, honesty in dealings, and care in managing the business.

In the end, the liability of LLC members and managers under the ULLCA reflects a balance between independence and responsibility. LLCs offer remarkable flexibility. They allow owners to draft operating agreements that suit their relationships. They protect personal assets from business losses. They welcome both active managers and passive investors. Yet they also enforce accountability where it matters: when individuals act wrongfully, break promises, blur lines, or misuse the structure. The stories of Blue Harbor Kayaks, Red Willow Ales, Silver Ridge Estates, Hearthstone Coffee Roasters, and others show how these doctrines play out in real life. They reveal how optimism, trust, negligence, ambition, or dishonesty can lead individuals toward liability or away from it. For students of business law, understanding these principles helps illuminate the powerful yet fragile nature of limited liability. It is both a shield and a responsibility, and the ULLCA makes clear that its protection must be earned through proper conduct.

Piercing the Veil

When people form corporations or limited liability companies, they often imagine the business as a kind of legal fortress—something that stands between them and personal financial ruin. This belief is mostly accurate. The entire modern business world depends on limited liability. It encourages people to take risks, innovate, and invest without fearing that a single mistake or downturn could cost them their home or their savings. Yet courts have always insisted that this protection has limits. When owners misuse the business form, treat it as a personal puppet, or use it to perpetrate wrongdoing, the fortress cracks. The court may pierce the corporate or LLC veil, reaching through the entity to hold owners personally responsible. This doctrine, often dramatic in application, is one of the most unpredictable and emotionally charged areas of business law. It sits at the intersection of fairness, morality, and economic structure, showing that the law will not allow people to hide behind a business shell when doing so would cause injustice.

When the Business and the Person Become Indistinguishable

The heart of veil piercing lies in the idea that a corporation or LLC must truly act as a separate being. It cannot simply be a disguise for the owner's personal affairs. When courts pierce the veil, they are declaring that the owner and the business have become indistinguishable, either through carelessness or deliberate misconduct.

Consider a small trucking business called SteelHawk Freight, formed as an LLC by its sole member, Derek. On paper, SteelHawk looks like a legitimate business. But Derek rarely respects the separation between himself and the company. All business funds go into the same checking account he uses for groceries, gas, vacations, and school tuition. He never prepares financial statements. He does not keep a minute book or maintain any records. He pays drivers in cash without documenting payroll. When creditors call, he alternates between saying "I owe you" and "the company owes you," depending on what sounds better at the moment. After a serious highway accident caused by one of his trucks leaves a motorist badly injured, SteelHawk is sued. But the LLC has almost no assets because Derek has drained money from the business for years.

In this scenario, veil piercing is not merely possible—it is likely. Courts see that Derek treated SteelHawk as an extension of himself. He blurred the line between personal and business affairs so thoroughly that honoring the legal separation would produce injustice. Veil piercing steps in not to punish Derek for being disorganized, but because his behavior undermined the integrity of the LLC form. When the separation between person and company disappears in practice, the law will not maintain that separation in court.

A similar story unfolds in a different industry. Imagine a family-owned restaurant called The Sunflower Bistro, incorporated by two siblings, Mara and Philip. They dream of passing the business to future generations. But the siblings commingle funds constantly. Mara buys furniture for her house using the restaurant's credit line. Philip uses corporate funds to make payments on his personal truck. They have no bylaws, no minutes, no payroll system, and no tax records beyond a shoebox of receipts. When a fire breaks out in the kitchen due to faulty wiring, destroying part of a neighboring business, multiple claims are filed. The corporation has almost no insurance and few assets because the siblings have treated it like a personal expense account. Once again, the court may pierce the veil because there is no meaningful corporate identity to shield.

These situations show the common thread: veil piercing often happens when the business lacks a genuine existence apart from its owners. The more the business behaves like a separate person—keeping records, maintaining accounts, following agreements—the stronger the liability shield. The more it collapses into the owner's personal life, the easier it becomes for courts to say that the separation is fictitious.

Using the Entity to Commit Fraud, Injustice, or Wrongdoing

Even if owners maintain some formalities, courts will pierce the veil when the entity is used to commit fraud or injustice. In these cases, the focus is not on whether records are messy but on whether the business form is being misused as a weapon or shield for improper conduct.

Imagine a property development corporation called Horizon Peak Builders, run by three investors. They create the corporation to construct affordable housing.

But behind the scenes, the investors use Horizon Peak to perform a different kind of project: siphoning funds from local lenders. They approach multiple small banks, promising to use loans for construction, but instead funnel the money into offshore accounts. They provide fraudulent receipts and stage construction photos. They even pour foundations in a few places to maintain appearances. When the lenders eventually discover the truth and sue, Horizon Peak claims it is bankrupt and cannot repay anything. In such a case, veil piercing is not just possible—it is almost inevitable. Courts will not allow fraudsters to hide behind a corporation to protect stolen money.

But not all veil piercing based on wrongdoing involves dramatic fraud. Sometimes it arises from quieter but equally damaging injustices. Consider a cleaning-services LLC called FreshStart Solutions, owned by a single member named Alex. FreshStart hires dozens of workers, paying them low wages and often missing paydays when cash flow is tight. Instead of paying the workers, Alex withdraws money from the business to support his lifestyle. Workers eventually sue for unpaid wages. FreshStart claims it has no funds, and indeed the company account is empty. But Alex has used the LLC as a shield to take money that should have gone to employees. A court may pierce the veil to make Alex personally liable because failing to do so would reward cynicism and harm vulnerable workers.

Another example involves creditors who rely on the

supposed independence of a business. Suppose a home-repair LLC called BrightSide Contracting advertises that it is fully insured, financially stable, and backed by years of experience. In reality, the owner, Simone, formed the LLC last month after declaring personal bankruptcy. She never buys insurance. She uses borrowed tools and hides the fact that BrightSide has no assets. When a customer's roof collapses after a botched repair job, Simone shuts down the LLC overnight, hoping to avoid liability. The court may pierce the veil because Simone misused the entity to deceive customers into believing they were dealing with a legitimate business.

The common thread in these examples is unfairness. Veil piercing exists to prevent owners from using limited liability as a tool of deceit, exploitation, or escape. Even small acts of injustice—hiding assets, misleading customers, draining the business before creditors can collect—can inspire courts to hold owners personally liable.

Undercapitalization, Control, and the Collapse of Fairness

A third major pathway to veil piercing involves undercapitalization and excessive control. Undercapitalization occurs when owners create a business without providing it with enough resources to meet foreseeable obligations. Excessive control occurs when owners treat the entity not merely as a business but as a puppet whose strings they pull without regard to corporate norms or the rights of others.

Imagine a biomedical start-up called Genexia Labs, formed by three scientists hoping to pioneer new diagnostics. They incorporate the business but invest only a few hundred dollars of their own money. They lease expensive equipment, take on large research contracts, and hire staff. When an experiment involving hazardous chemicals ends in an accident, Genexia faces millions in liability. The corporation claims it cannot pay because it has almost no capital. The law may pierce the veil because the founders created an entity destined to fail its obligations. Undercapitalization signals that the corporation was never meant to be a true buffer; it was a shell for risky activities.

A less dramatic but equally instructive scenario comes from the world of family businesses. Suppose a farm supply LLC called Golden Valley Feed is owned by an older couple, Ronald and Patricia. They treat the LLC as a family project but never separate its finances from their personal accounts. Ronald uses LLC funds to pay personal debts. Patricia uses her personal account to pay LLC bills. They sign personal checks on behalf of the company and company checks on behalf of themselves. Employees, suppliers, and customers cannot tell where the business ends and the couple begins. When the LLC fails and cannot pay suppliers, the suppliers argue that the LLC was never a genuine entity. Courts may pierce the veil because of excessive control and blurred boundaries.

Undercapitalization and excessive control often work together. A business without meaningful capital is unhealthy from the start. A business run like a personal slush fund is structurally unsound. Courts look for patterns: misuse of funds, absence of records, domination by a single member, failure to follow agreements, and behavior that misleads third parties about the company's true nature. When these patterns converge, the rationale for limited liability dissolves, and personal liability arises as a form of legal correction.

In the end, veil piercing remains one of the most dramatic and unpredictable doctrines in business law. Courts use it sparingly, with caution, because limited liability is the foundation of modern commerce. But when the corporate or LLC form is abused—through commingling, fraud, injustice, undercapitalization, or domination—courts will not hesitate to remove the shield. The doctrine serves as a reminder that business entities, while powerful, demand responsible stewardship. They require owners to respect boundaries, honor obligations, and maintain separation between their personal and business lives. When those boundaries collapse, so does the protection they once provided. Veil piercing stands as a last-resort tool to ensure fairness, integrity, and accountability in the world of business associations.

11 THE CORE LESSONS OF BUSINESS ASSOCIATIONS

When we step back from the dense rules, cases, and doctrines of business associations, a simple truth emerges: every business relationship is built on trust, power, and responsibility. The law of agency, partnerships, corporations, and limited liability companies exists not to complicate these relationships, but to shape them, channel them, and make them predictable. It gives language to loyalty, boundaries to authority, and consequences to choices. This concluding chapter pulls together the most important lessons from our journey through the world of business associations—a reminder of what matters most when people build, manage, and rely on business entities.

The foundation of everything begins with agency. The law of agency tells us how one person can act on behalf of another and make decisions that legally bind the principal. We learned that agency relationships arise when a principal manifests an intention for an agent to act on the principal's behalf and under the principal's control, and the agent consents. That simple structure fuels nearly every business form that follows. A single real estate agent negotiating a sale, a cashier completing a transaction, a CEO signing a contract—all are agents whose actions carry legal consequences for someone else. Agency law emphasizes that authority can take different forms. Actual authority grows out of communication between principal and agent, while apparent authority arises from what the principal communicates to third parties. Distinguishing between the two is vital because it determines who bears responsibility when expectations collide.

These distinctions matter because an agent's actions can expose the principal to liability, even when the principal never intended the agent to take that particular step. Agency law also establishes the agent's fiduciary duties to the principal, especially the duties of care and loyalty. These duties remind us that agency relationships involve more than instructions—they involve trust. An agent must act with competence, keep the principal informed, and put the principal's interests above their own. Likewise, an agent's duties to third parties reflect fairness: liability depends on whether the principal is disclosed, partially disclosed, or undisclosed, and these categories shape who bears the risk of misunderstanding. The law's consistent theme is that clarity in agency relationships protects everyone involved.

From agency, we moved to vicarious liability, a doctrine that often catches newcomers by surprise. A principal may be held liable for the torts of an agent or employee, even when the principal did nothing wrong personally. This principle—respondeat superior—rests on the idea that people who benefit from an enterprise should also bear its costs. Liability depends on whether the agent was acting within the scope of employment, whether the relationship was that of employer–employee or independent contractor, and whether the principal exercised control. The distinctions can feel fine-grained, but the stories we explored showed how real-life situations push the boundaries. When a delivery driver rushes to meet a deadline or when a franchise employee blurs the lines between corporate branding and independent discretion, the question becomes: who should ultimately bear responsibility for the harm? Vicarious liability answers that question by following control, benefit, and fairness.

These ideas lead naturally into the world of partnerships. Unlike corporations or LLCs, partnerships arise easily—sometimes too easily. Two people agreeing to carry on a business for profit become partners whether or not they intended to create a formal legal relationship. This low barrier makes partnerships flexible but also dangerous. Under the Revised Uniform Partnership Act, every general partner has broad authority to bind the partnership in the ordinary course of business, and every partner is personally liable for the debts and obligations of the partnership. The stories we explored—friends opening a bakery or cousins launching a lawn-care business—showed how meaningful this rule is. Partnerships depend on trust and clarity. A single partner's decision can obligate all partners, even on matters they never discussed. That is why partnership agreements matter so deeply; they shape management, control, profit sharing, dissociation, and dissolution. Whether a partnership is at-will or formed for a definite term determines how easily a partner may withdraw. And when a partner's behavior triggers dissolution—whether orderly or chaotic—the law steps in to guide the winding up of the business.

From partnerships, we turned to the formation of corporations and LLCs, learning that formality and structure play far greater roles when people seek clearer boundaries and stronger protection. Corporations require articles of incorporation, bylaws, and thoughtful governance frameworks. These documents outline the corporation's purpose, internal rules, classes of stock, and the rights of shareholders. Amendments require careful procedures, reflecting the corporation's status as an independent legal entity—one that will outlive its founders. LLCs, by contrast, are built on flexibility. Their chartering documents vary by jurisdiction, and their operating agreements—whether written, oral, or implied by conduct—serve as the central tool for tailoring the business's internal rules. These agreements can shape voting rights, management structures, profit allocations, fiduciary duties, and exit strategies. The difference between corporations and LLCs reflects a philosophical divide: corporations impose structure for stability, while LLCs invite creativity for adaptability.

Before a corporation even exists, however, promoters play a crucial role. Their actions often determine whether a business starts on solid footing or stumbles from the beginning. Promoters enter into contracts, secure financing, and negotiate leases—but because the corporation does not yet exist, a promoter may be personally liable unless the corporation later adopts or ratifies the contract. Promoters also owe fiduciary duties to the future corporation, meaning they must avoid conflicts of interest, disclose all material information, and refrain from self-dealing. The stories we explored—entrepreneurs juggling leases, investors, and enthusiasm—show how easily promoters can slip into risky territory. The law emphasizes responsibility, transparency, and fairness to protect the fragile moment when a business is still only an idea.

With formation complete, we examined management and control of corporations and LLCs. Corporations divide power among shareholders, directors, and officers. Shareholders elect directors, vote on major transactions, and exercise rights shaped by notice, quorum, and proxy rules. Directors oversee the corporation's strategic direction, acting through meetings, committees, or written consents. Officers handle the day-to-day operations, wielding authority that binds the corporation when exercised properly. These layers of governance distribute power in a way that ensures accountability and stability. In contrast, LLCs provide fluid management structures, allowing businesses to choose between member-managed or manager-managed models. Members and managers can customize their roles through operating agreements, reflecting personal relationships and business priorities. But even in this flexible environment, certain rights and duties remain mandatory, emphasizing that private ordering has its limits.

All these structures depend on trust, which brought us to fiduciary duties. General partners owe the highest duties of loyalty and care, given the intimate and collaborative nature of partnerships. Corporate officers and directors operate under the business judgment rule, which protects good-faith decisions but imposes liability for conflicts of interest, bad faith, or intentional misconduct. LLC members and managers occupy a middle ground where duties may be shaped—and sometimes modified—by the operating agreement, but cannot be eliminated entirely when doing so would undermine fundamental fairness. Across all business forms, fiduciary duties ensure that people entrusted with power use it responsibly. They prevent self-dealing, dishonesty, negligence, and abuse of authority. The law does not require perfection, but it demands integrity.

Shareholder and member litigation provides the enforcement mechanism for these duties. Direct actions allow individuals to protect personal rights, such as voting or access to information. Derivative actions empower shareholders or members to step into the business's shoes and pursue claims that the entity itself has failed to enforce. Understanding who is suing whom—and for what—is essential. These suits emphasize that businesses, though composed of individuals, maintain distinct identities and rights. Derivative litigation protects the business from internal wrongdoing, while direct litigation protects individual investors from personal harm. Together, they maintain balance within the entity.

All these doctrines converge in the final subject: liability rules related to business associations. General partners face sweeping personal liability under RUPA, bearing responsibility for the partnership's obligations simply by virtue of being partners. Corporate officers and directors face liability only when they engage in misconduct, intentional wrongdoing, or breach their duties. LLC members and managers enjoy strong limited liability protections, but can lose them when they personally commit torts, guarantee obligations, or undermine the integrity of the entity. And piercing the veil—one of the most dramatic remedies in business law—reminds us that limited liability is a privilege, not a right. When owners commingle funds, undercapitalize entities, commit fraud, or use the business form to avoid fairness, courts may reach through the entity to impose personal responsibility.

Across all these topics, one theme repeats itself: business associations are built on relationships. Relationships between principals and agents, partners and partners, directors and shareholders, members and managers, businesses and the people who rely on them. The doctrines we studied are not isolated rules—they are interconnected tools designed to manage risk, protect trust, and align incentives. They ensure that when people act together to pursue economic goals, they do so within a framework that encourages honesty, responsibility, and fairness.

As you finish this book, the most important lesson to carry forward is that business law is not just technical; it is human. It reflects optimism and ambition, but also caution and accountability. It allows people to dream big while still recognizing that power must be used with care. Whether you are studying for the bar exam, entering practice, or simply exploring the structure of business life, remember that every doctrine you learned is rooted in a simple question: how can people work together in a way that is fair, efficient, and just?

ABOUT THE AUTHOR

Jordan K. Fairfield has devoted more than twenty-five years to the practice and teaching of law, building a career grounded in clarity, compassion, and a deep commitment to helping others approach legal study with confidence. With a broad and varied background in legal practice, Jordan brings a practical perspective to teaching—one shaped by years of advising clients, resolving disputes, and navigating the real-world pressures that give legal rules their meaning. This practical orientation informs each of Jordan's teaching projects, transforming complex material into clear explanations enriched by experience and insight.

Beyond the world of practice, Jordan has spent many years teaching in both law schools and paralegal programs, guiding students from their first days of legal study through advanced coursework. Known for an accessible and empathetic teaching style, Jordan excels at breaking down difficult concepts without oversimplifying them, making challenging subjects feel manageable and engaging. That same approach underlies this book and the larger series it introduces: learning the law should be intellectually demanding, but never demoralizing.

Jordan's dedication to supporting future legal professionals extends to bar preparation as well. Over the years, Jordan has provided individualized bar tutoring and mentorship to students across the country. More than one hundred aspiring attorneys have successfully passed the bar exam with Jordan's support—a testament to both deep expertise and a sincere commitment to each student's success.

This book reflects the accumulation of those decades of experience: thousands of hours in practice, the classroom, and one-on-one tutoring sessions. It is written with the hope that readers—whether studying for an exam, beginning a course, or seeking a clearer understanding of the legal landscape—will find encouragement, clarity, and a welcoming path into the study of law.

If you found this book useful—and especially if it helped you to pass the bar exam—please email to celebrate your success!

jordan.k.fairfield@gmail.com